MIME
Basics for Beginners

MIME

Basics for Beginners

CINDIE
and
MATTHEW STRAUB

Photography by JEFF BLANTON

Boston   PLAYS, INC.   *Publishers*

Library of Congress Cataloging in Publication Data

Straub, Cindie.
    Mime: basics for beginners.

    Includes index.
    Summary: Basic instruction for those interested in
learning mime.   Includes photographs.
    1. Mime—Juvenile literature.   [1. Pantomime]
I. Straub, Matthew.   II. Title.
PN2071.G4S87   1984   792.3   84-11694
ISBN 0-8238-0263-9

Printed in the United States of America

CONTENTS

To Louis E. Straub

MIME
Basics for Beginners

A Brief History of Mime

THE earliest and most primitive forms of Mime were performed by hunters and warriors who moved, gestured, danced, and acted out their stories and feelings as a means of communication.

The first use of pantomimes in recorded history occurred in India in the 5th century B.C. Entertainers, singers, dancers, and mimes would perform for Bharatta, the god of "Dramatic Presentation." The Hindu dramatic writer, Babhavnti, wrote pantomimes into his plays.

Around the 4th century B.C. the use of pantomime began to spread along the trading routes east to China, where performers used Mime to tell stories of social and historic events.

By the early 6th century A.D., the Japanese had discovered what was by then the well established theater form of the Chinese. They, too, used pantomimes to perform for the gods and tell epic tales of war and history, and they developed "Sambaso," a pantomime to prevent earthquakes and volcanic eruptions.

In both the Chinese and Japanese cultures, Mime performance has continued to the present day, not as a single, discrete art form, but as an integral part of the overall performance, inseparable from the dancing, acting, and music.

In its theatrical form, Mime traveled west by way of the mystery plays of Egypt and ancient Greece. In 4th century B.C. Greece, what we know as pantomimes were referred to as ethologues, meaning "portrayal of manners." An ethologue provided a short introduction to the main performance, and in between acts, it gave comic relief to the audience and a rest for the actors in the play. These pantomimes were undeveloped in form, featuring messages and skits based on moral lessons and everyday activities. Music—most likely flute—accompanied the performance.

With the passage of time, Mime evolved into a form in which actors performed silent dramas: pantomimes that emphasized the character rather than the plot. The actors wore either half masks or full masks with no hole for the mouth, to let the audience know they would be watching a pantomime, or "dumb show."

One of the first Greek pantomimes introduced to the Roman stage took place in southern Italy at the Festival of Flora, a pre-Christian Roman festival similar to the riotous Greek festival of Dionysus. Because Mime was unfamiliar to audiences in Italy, a performer offstage may have narrated the action while the mime pantomimed his words.

During the Middle Ages, mime was used extensively by the traveling jester, who was probably the forerunner of the comic mime solo performer of today. Mime also remained a part of Church-approved religious morality plays, though these were much more religious than the ancient Greek form. In the sixteenth century, Mime was brought back to the stage and into the streets with Commedia dell'Arte, a form of traveling theater performing short vignettes, and using speech and pantomime to give comic relief. This rustic and simple art form used much physical action and followed established and easily recognized conventions, with stock characters. In 1576, an Italian company of players, led by Flamino Scala, traveled to France and introduced Mime to the royal courts. The French developed the form into the familiar Harlequin, which still survives today.

By 1800, Mime had become a familiar medium for dramatic entertainment in many countries, but it was in the early nineteenth century that popular Mime as we know it today began with the work of Jean Gaspard Deburau. Deburau transformed what had once been a crude, slapstick art form into real theater; he created stories with realistic scenes, fully-developed characters, and plots about everyday life. He also created the popular character of Pierrot, the lovesick, pale, attractive mime in flowing white costume and black skull cap.

When Deburau died, his son Charles took his place in the theater and began the formal teaching of Mime as a systemized technique. Mime was so well received that Deburau's students would perform one-act pantomimes at the Paris Opera.

After World War I, at the Vieux Colombier school, Jacques Copeau continued the teaching of traditional French Mime to many students, among them Etienne Decroux, who went on to create a modern system of Mime technique with theories, exercises, and specific illusions. One of Decroux's students has inspired an international enthusiasm for Mime. That world-famous mime is Marcel Marceau.

Marceau's style of Mime is based on exacting physical technique and the "sculpting" of space. He portrays the essence of a situation with simple, cleanly drawn movements; and he has brought new meaning and dimension to the world of Mime with his lovable character, Mr. Bip. Mr. Bip, with his recognizable top hat and flower, is Everyman, thrown into a thousand situations and circumstances.

With over 300 performances a year, all over the world, Marceau continues to delight hundreds of thousands of people with his modern rendering of a tradition of theater spanning 2,500 years.

Introduction

Mime: Basics for Beginners is a workbook. It is not a philosophic statement, not a history, nor is it an exposition of "new" directions in Mime.

It teaches "traditional" Mime: Mime as a distinct art form not linked to any of the techniques often associated with it—juggling, dance, fire eating—and using few masks and props.

Mime: Basics for Beginners teaches fundamentals of the traditional Mime styles that most people are familiar with, and that involve whiteface make-up and costume, background music, a silent actor, and exact body motions and gestures (mostly traditional Mime illusions) conveying specific meanings. The pantomime, which is the "story" the performer acts out, may follow a traditional story line or explore an abstract theme.

The aim of this book is to help beginners become confident performers of Mime, whatever the style. (Unfortunately, the only agreement among mimes is a general *disagreement* over what "Mime" actually is.) Here is a brief summary of the Mime styles found in America, Europe, and Asia:

Corporeal Mime, commonly referred to as the French style of Mime, was developed by Etienne Decroux in the early part of the

20th century. Corporeal Mime has a very technical movement vocabulary, and it requires extensive training. Facial expressions are de-emphasized in favor of the body, which makes a strong, serious statement.

Asian style of Mime relies heavily on make-up and costumes. In Chinese, Japanese, and Indian theater, Mime is an integral part of many kinds of performances, inseparable from dance and acting. The performances include many gymnastic movements—flips, etc.—and the elaborate costumes and make-up suggest immediately characters with whom the audiences are familiar.

American Mime is a specific style of Mime created by Paul Curtis and practiced by the American Mime Theater in New York City. Props and masks are used sparingly, if at all. Black unitards are used as costumes. The pantomimes do not follow traditional story lines with specific plots but develop abstract themes and present series of images that explore emotional states and leave the audience with a certain feeling. Voice is used when the script calls for a word, phrase or noise.

Of course, an individual mime can develop his own, unique style; he may or may not wear make-up, for instance, and may choose to incorporate dance or slapstick into a pantomime. As for costumes, some mimes feature the bizarre and may wear a box as a mask or work from inside a large sack.

Still other mimes may practice a "robot" style, in which movements are stiff, mechanical. Again, make-up is optional, and though each performer's costume is unique, it must be designed so that the mime can easily make the rigid and angular movements that characterize this original style.

Many performers who are not mimes—jugglers, clowns, dancers, even guitar players—have discovered ways to incorporate Mime effectively into their performances. In addition, Mime "bit roles" are used frequently in television situation comedies, motion pictures, or stage drama, in which the script calls for one of the characters (an actor with lines) to create a role using Mime. For example, if directions in a script call for a character to "mime" a telephone call, the actor will pick up an imaginary receiver, mime a conversation, then hang up.

These are just some of the dozens of ways that Mime has become an important part of the world of entertainment today. As many facets as there are to the world of Mime, the beginnings for all styles are the same: development of body control, attitude toward image, a sense of characterization and script, and stage presence. Instructing Mime students in these elements is the purpose of *Mime: Basics for Beginners*. As the aspiring mime develops his artistic sense, he will clarify and refine his own unique approach to this fundamental and widely varied art form.

THE units that make up this book are designed for students working on their own to become Mime performers. If the student is thorough and "trains," mastering the exercises as an athlete masters a sport, the apprenticeship can be compressed into several weeks. On the other hand, the study can be continued over several years at a more leisurely pace—as long as the student continually develops fresh material and keeps up the physical work and practice on a regular basis.

The units in this book should be studied in the sequence given. The first units deal with the important physical exercises needed for Mime performance. Later units are designed to help the mime develop the creative aspects: creating an image, characterization, improvisation, and playwriting.

The text begins with essential Mime definitions (Unit 1) and basic physical exercises (Unit 2). Unit 3 describes in detail the five basic body positions and motion exercises that are essential for any work in Mime, and Unit 4, Moving Illusions, covers longer movement sequences that can actually serve as short Mime performances.

Unit 5, Characterization and Character, and Unit 6, Playwriting, teach the aspiring mime to write his own performance material—a necessity, in view of the lack of good published pantomime scripts. Unit 7 describes rehearsal techniques, Unit 8 (Make-up and Costume) explains the "how-to" of a mime's visual appearance, and Unit

9, Performance, shows the mime how to present his carefully rehearsed movements before a live audience.

In all of the exercises, the student mime must constantly be aware of correct basic Mime positions, and refer to illustrations and photographs repeatedly until he or she has mastered them. It is advisable to correct any deficiencies in a particular position or movement before going on to the next.

For purposes of simplicity, the pronouns "he" and "him" are used generically, instead of the clumsy and repetitive constructions of "he and she" and "him and her." It is understood that mimes can be either male or female and very often the role is "neutral," neither male or female.

A full-length mirror and adequate practice area are essential for serious Mime work.

Mime is a physical art; it requires stamina and continuous physical training. Therefore, each practice session should include the Isolation Exercises and Motion Exercises, as well as specific Unit material.

UNIT 1

Stage Mime, Street Mime

Stage Mime, Street Mime

MIME is for everyone who wants to explore an art form that is ancient yet modern; has no language barriers; is good, healthy exercise; and offers a personal challenge to create "something out of nothing." Even experienced performers in the other arts will find in Mime the freedom that comes from having no props, bulky sets, or strictly written scripts to control them. Unfettered by extension cords, a mime can take his show any place—indoors or out, formal stage, TV studio, hospital room, or park—and find an appreciative audience.

And the only expenditures required are for make-up and the simplest of costumes.

MIME, MIME, AND PANTOMIME

The beginning Mime student needs to learn a few definitions, because there is much disagreement and confusion over the meanings of terms used in Mime. For the purposes of this book, *Mime* (capital "M") refers to the art form: the world of Mime. The word *mime* (lower case "m") refers to the practitioner, the performer who employs the principles of Mime in making his illusions. *Pantomime* refers to the shows, stories, and "events" presented by the mime.

If a performing mime picks an imaginary flower, he has created a Mime illusion using standard techniques of Mime. If the performer goes on to do something with the flower, he then has developed a story, a pantomime. A *mime* uses the techniques of *Mime* to portray *pantomimes*.

Most mimes will agree on these general definitions, possibly with some qualifications.

STREET MIME AND STAGE MIME

Mime performance, broadly speaking, is presented in two different forms: Street Mime and Stage Mime.

Street Mime refers to any performance that is not staged and plotted out in advance. This spontaneous form of Mime uses much on-the-spot improvisation. Street Mime usually involves working in a crowd. The mime may move through the crowd, improvising and performing as he goes, or he may station himself in one place and let the crowd flow past him as he performs. As the mime confronts each new "audience," he reaches for laughter and other positive emotional reactions.

The advantage of Street Mime is that the mime has total mobility. Unhampered by the boundaries of a stage, a mime is free to perform any place he can gather an interested crowd. Every street corner, sidewalk, restaurant, park, shopping mall, lawn, church basement, rotunda, meeting hall, department store, birthday party, schoolroom, day care center, parking lot, art show, retirement center, backyard, house party, cafeteria, etc., offers a possible performance site.

Street Mime can be exciting. The mime never knows who the immediate audience will be. The onlookers are always changing as new people join the crowd. As the mime presents himself to each new group, he must rely on his creative improvisation to tell a story, however simple, and leave the audience satisfied. He then quickly moves on to the next audience. The mime may interact with a single person as the focus for a larger audience of onlookers, or address a couple or a family unit.

How the mime varies his street performance depends on the nature of the crowd. Much forethought must be given to the performing area and the kind of crowd likely to gather. A seated theater audience is more predictable. A street crowd is complex: Some individuals are rushing to lunch, while others are looking at squirrels with their children. Some of the children are happy, some are tired, affecting how they react to a mime, and, in turn, how a mime acts for them. Lunchtime audiences and Friday afternoon crowds are often preoccupied. The way a street mime works each crowd depends on his sensitivity to the nature of the audience, and to time limitation, and his ability to adjust his performance accordingly.

In Street Mime, there is less pressure to tell a full story and more dependence on "object" miming. A beginning mime can use the easiest illusions. Close up, the hands and face come into greater play; stage performance requires more complicated, whole-body movements.

Street performances demand boundless energy, and the mime must be adaptable and able to react quickly, requiring imagination and creativity. As he moves through the everchanging crowd, the mime has great opportunity for intimate, one-to-one interaction. Few art forms offer this flexibility.

With such seeming freedom for performing, the potential pitfalls in Street Mime may not be immediately apparent: People in the crowd may reach out and touch the performer or intrude on the performance to take pictures or make comments. Sudden noises or interruptions may distract the mime and destroy the illusions.

The limitations of Street Mime bring a greater appreciation of the depth and complexity of stage work. A mime with no previous experience performing in front of an audience, can gain experience and confidence and develop his own style by doing Street Mime. Experience in Street Mime provides the foundation for later performance in Stage Mime. The aspiring mime learns how to cover any mistakes, develops a sense of timing, works out routines and themes, and brings together all the skills needed to give a sustained stage performance.

Stage Mime offers a more predictable and controlled performing situation, because the performer is separated from the audience by the stage and all attention is focused on him. Such theatrical aids as lighting, sound, and music enhance the performance. Also, the people in the audience have chosen to be there and know generally what to expect of the performance.

This permits the mime to prepare and give a more complicated performance. A stage mime can present longer and more sustained illusions, and tell a much richer, fuller tale. He may portray deeper characterizations and present a more intricate pantomime. Viewed at a greater distance than in a street performance, he can build a rapport with a stable audience over a longer period of time, without interference or interruption that occurs constantly in Street Mime.

A stage mime must have energy and stamina in order to present convincingly the large number of illusions (all interesting and technically well prepared) needed for a full program that may last as long as two hours.

Because of the lack of available material, a stage mime must be able to write and create his own repertoire. The mime must understand completely the characterization, plot line, pacing, and timing in the story and be familiar with all aspects of the material he has created, so that he can perform with competence and confidence.

In addition, the stage mime must plan the sound and lighting support he wants, and make the necessary cue sheets. He must spend extra practice time coordinating these light-and-sound cues with the technicians and the script.

Well-made, artistic title cards are a must for Stage Mime. No one likes a tacky or amateurish introduction to a performance. (The titles should not be spoken by the mime, as this breaks the mood of the mime's silent characterization.)

As the beginning mime becomes more skilled and experienced, he gets a feel for what works best for his style and personality. He incorporates and develops his ideas into stories, and with a growing understanding of performance, he turns these stories into pantomimes, schedules his stage performances with a particular audience in mind, coordinates lighting and sound, works out title cards, and so on.

UNIT 2

The Body in "Parts"

The Body in "Parts"

ALL work in Mime starts with good, basic body control. But before the first move is made, proper breathing and proper beginning posture must be understood.

DIAPHRAGMATIC BREATHING

Proper breath control is the foundation of any successful Mime activity. Chest breathing with its tenseness and tightness cannot provide the energy and relaxation a physical performer needs, whether he be a mime, dancer, singer, musician, or an athlete.

The superior mode of breathing uses the strength of the diaphragm. The diaphragm is the partition of muscles and tendons between the chest cavity and abdominal cavity. It directly controls your lungs. By using the diaphragm for breathing, you can keep your chest relaxed and free to expand to its fullest limit. A deep sigh is simple diaphragmatic breathing.

THE DIAPHRAGM

21

The following exercises will help you understand this natural way of breathing and will train you in its use.

1. Lie on the floor, on your back, and place your palms over your diaphragm (just under your rib cage).

Breathe "from your stomach."

Feel your palms rise and fall as your diaphragm expands and contracts with each breath.

This is the proper way to breathe while doing Mime.

2. Lie on your back and place one or more heavy books on the diaphragm area.

Slowly inhale and exhale. Watch the books move up and down.

Repeat many times. Notice the calming effect this type of breathing produces.

3. Try this exercise with a partner. Stand erect, though relaxed, with your back flat against a wall. Have your partner face you and place his fists, close together, directly below your rib cage, so that his index fingers rest at the edge of your ribs.

Have your partner lean against you so that his weight is being supported by your diaphragm.

As he slowly leans toward you, inhale, thus gently pushing him away.

Exhale, and he will lean toward you.

Continue breathing as you gently rock him back and forth.

Practice these diaphragmatic breathing exercises until this motion becomes natural and automatic.

Diaphragmatic breathing is basic to the Mime activities that follow; it will give your body the energy and relaxation you need to create believable illusions.

Neutral Position

First you must learn the *neutral position*, which is the basis for all positions and movements in Mime work.

Begin by standing up straight. Place your heels four or five inches apart, feet at a 45-degree angle. Relax—especially your chest and back.

Raise your body from its center by breathing with the diaphragm.

Imagine a magnet lifting you from the crown of your head.

Think of each section of your body as if it were independent, with just enough spinal muscular energy to keep the whole structure erect.

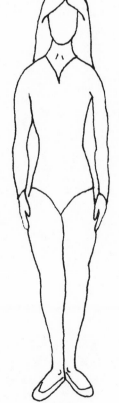

NEUTRAL POSITION

23

ISOLATION

After diaphragmatic breathing and neutral position have been mastered, you must turn your attention to the series of physical exercises called Isolation Exercises. These exercises are essential to give you a sense of your body elements and the ways you can make these elements respond predictably and precisely. The word Isolation, as used in Mime, means the study of the individual parts or sections of the body, isolating each one from the others to allow you to work on that area alone.

The body must be precisely controlled by the mime, either in whole or in part, or in any combination of these parts. These combinations are the building blocks of all Mime positions. You must learn to make every part of your body respond exactly (and repeatedly) to your mental commands.

Example: Freeze right where you are. If you are seated, you have commanded your body to sit. But you did so unconsciously, automatically, without any awareness of the hundreds of muscle contractions and minute adjustments and changes in balance involved in the process of moving your body into a sitting position. Analyze the position you are in: Are both feet flat on the floor? Toes curled under? Back hunched? Shoulders curved inward? Is your head tilted to one side, or is it jutting forward, ducklike?

To gain conscious control of your movements, you must practice Isolation Exercises with each body part.

Maintain relaxed diaphragmatic breathing as you do the following Isolation Exercises.

Standing in neutral position, imagine that your body is divided into nine sections: head, neck, shoulders, chest, arms, pelvis, knees, feet, and face.

1. Isolation of the head

Starting in neutral position, isolate your head. Rotate it, keeping your spinal column motionless.

Slowly tilt the head to the left. Keep your neck straight, but not stiff.

HEAD ISOLATION

Bring your head up straight to neutral position again.

Now slowly tilt to the right.

Return to neutral position.

Repeat. Continue breathing with your diaphragm throughout the exercise.

Next, roll your head from the top of your spine in a clockwise motion, smoothly and evenly. Do not move your neck.

Return to neutral position.

Now, roll your head counterclockwise.

Return to neutral position.

Repeat. Work toward isolation and smoothness.

2. Isolation of the neck

From neutral position, push your chin out and down with your neck. Continue pushing until your chin rests in the "V" of your throat. Do not let your mouth drop open.

Repeat. Is the rest of your body relaxed in neutral position? Did you remember to breathe?

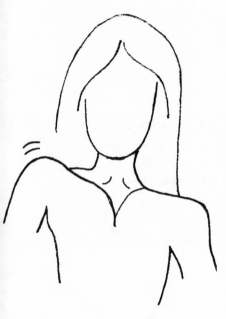

SHOULDER ISOLATION

3. Isolation of the shoulders

From neutral position, first roll your left shoulder in a downward motion. Do not move your neck or chest. Return to neutral position.

Repeat several times, checking your position in a mirror.

Do the same isolation slowly with your right shoulder, once again making sure that with the shoulder motion you do not also move your chest or neck. Breathe with diaphragm throughout this movement.

Repeat.

From a relaxed neutral position, roll both shoulders simultaneously in a circular motion: in, up, and back. Check your positioning in a mirror. Are your chest and neck always at rest?

Repeat several times.

4. Isolation of the chest

Starting from a relaxed neutral position, place your hands on hips. Expand your rib cage outward, breathing from your diaphragm.

Contract your rib cage. Breathe.

Repeat. Do not move the other sections of your body, especially the neck and waist.

5. Isolation of the arms

Good arm isolation is crucial for a convincing Mime performance. If Mime is to be more than "acting without words," then precise arm, elbow, and hand control is required for creating believable illusions. For example, "walls" must appear "solid" by repeated, exact hand positioning. Unwavering hand and finger placement is the essence of any hand illusion, whether it is a water glass or a bowling ball.

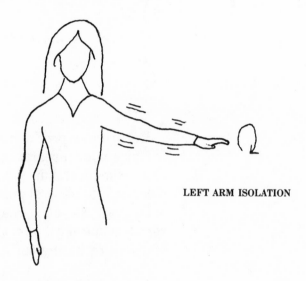

LEFT ARM ISOLATION

Left, full-arm isolation. Starting from the neutral position, isolate your left arm: stretch it out straight from the shoulder, parallel to the floor.

Rotate the whole arm from the shoulder in a clockwise motion, making a circle the size of a basketball.

Return to neutral position.

Raise your arm again and rotate it counter clockwise.

Return to neutral position.

As you repeat these motions, check to be sure that all other body elements remain at rest. Remember to continue regular, rhythmic breathing throughout.

Left forearm isolation. With your left arm parallel to the floor, allow your forearm to dangle from your elbow.

Rotate your forearm—without moving the upper half of your arm—in a clockwise circle the diameter of a basketball.

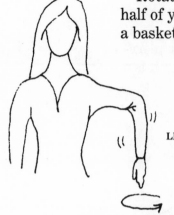

LEFT FOREARM ISOLATION

Return to a precise neutral position.

Raise your forearm again and rotate it in a counterclockwise direction.

Return to neutral position.

Repeat. As you repeat this exercise, check in a mirror to make sure you are holding your shoulder and elbow at right angles.

Left wrist isolation. With your upper left arm parallel to the floor and your left forearm exactly perpendicular, rotate your left hand clockwise, in a smooth motion. Return to neutral position, then repeat exercise, counterclockwise. Drop your left arm to your side in neutral position.

Check to make sure all body angles remain correct and relaxed throughout the entire arm isolation routine. Is your diaphragmatic breathing becoming easier and more automatic?

Repeat this entire series of arm isolation exercises with your right arm. Remember: Precision is the goal.

6. Isolation of the pelvis

Stand in neutral position with both arms extended straight from your shoulders to the side, parallel to the floor.

Rotate your hips clockwise, then reverse, in counterclockwise motion.

Repeat, then return to neutral position. When performing this exercise, it is important to keep other body elements at rest. With practice, this will become easier and more accurate.

PELVIS ISOLATION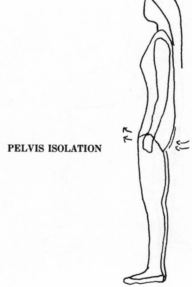

7. Isolation of the legs

Since maintaining balance is the most difficult task in this isolation exercise, it might be helpful at first to use a balancing bar or the back of a chair for temporary support.

Starting from neutral position, extend your left upper leg out to the side of your body, bending your knee so that the calf and foot are extended downward, pointing to the floor (similar to the position of the arm in the forearm isolation exercise).

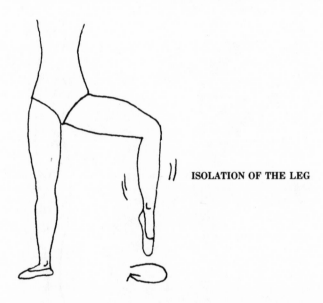

ISOLATION OF THE LEG

Slowly rotate the calf and foot from the knee, clockwise, drawing a circle the size of a basketball.

Do several revolutions.

Return to neutral position.

Repeat exercise with your right leg.

8. Isolation of the foot

Standing in neutral position, raise your left heel off the floor and stand on the ball and toes only.

Raise the ball of your left foot so that only the tips of toes are touching the floor. Now return to neutral position, rolling foot back—first bring the ball of your foot back to the floor, then the heel.

Continue this pattern of heel, ball, toe and the reverse: toe, ball, heel.

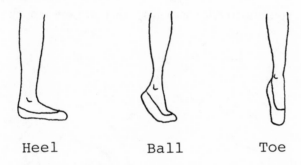

Heel   Ball   Toe

Repeat the routine, while making sure each action is clean and direct. Keep all weight on your right leg and foot; all other parts of your body remain in neutral position.

Repeat the foot isolation with the right foot, keeping all the weight of your body on your left leg and foot. Guard against unsteadiness and excess foot motion.

Because isolation of the foot is essential for mastering the Mime Walk, it is important to work on this exercise until you are sure you have mastered the technique.

9. Isolation of the face

Lips. While maintaining a relaxed neutral position, push your chin out from your face while turning under your lower lip.

From that position, slowly turn your lip up and down several times. Keep the chin as still as possible and relax the rest of your face.

Return to neutral position.

With the lips closed, tighten the corners of your mouth, as in a tight smile.

Move only the corners of your mouth up and down. You should be able to feel the muscles in the corners of your upper lip working as you perform this isolation.

LIP ISOLATION

From the same neutral position, pull the tension in your lips from one side to the other repeatedly. Is the action free and smooth, without any eyebrow movements?

Nose. From neutral position, concentrate on isolating your nose from the rest of your face. This isolation requires use of your upper lip muscles. To begin, push your upper lip muscles up, as in a "sniff" position, crinkling the skin on your nose.

Repeat the isolation exercise several times, then return to neutral position.

Eyes. In neutral position, move your eyes from side to side.

Move both eyes in an up-and-down pattern.

Finally, rotate your eyes clockwise, then counter-clockwise.

Repeat and return to neutral position.

Eyelids. Starting with your body and face in neutral position, slowly move your upper eyelids downward until they are completely closed.

Repeat, and return to neutral position.

Eyebrows. To isolate the eyebrows, work the muscles both above and below your eyebrows, moving your eyebrows up and down. Keep your mouth still and relaxed. Try to work each eyebrow individually.

Repeat, and return to neutral position.

Full face. For full-face isolation, drop your lower jaw and raise your eyebrows. Stretch your face as far as possible, keeping lip and cheek muscles relaxed.

Repeat.

The entire isolation exercise series is considered a "warm-up" routine and *should be performed every day* before any Mime performance is attempted.

After you have completed all isolation exercises, it is important to "shake out" your body.

Muscle tension is the primary element of Mime movement. The mime tenses only specific muscles, while keeping his body generally relaxed. This gives "reality" to the Mime movement and to the illusion being created.

While practicing the previous isolations, you may have noted a lack of "content." The isolation exercises alone are studies in "form." Tensed muscles add a dynamic to the action and are the basis for conveying real emotions to the audience.

Tensed muscles are obvious in the portrayals of such emotions as fear, anger, joy, and sadness. In sadness, for example, the theatrical exaggeration of a protruding lower lip and drawn-in shoulders immediately expresses the image of sadness to the audience.

Performing the isolation exercises with proper muscle tension—concentrating on each part of the body separately and in different combinations—also gives the mime a greater sense and awareness of his body.

By the simple addition of tension to the original isolation exercises, they are transformed into the fundamental, exaggerated, stylized movements that comprise the vocabulary of Mime.

Tension applied to isolation. Repeat the previous isolation exercises with this new instruction: Add muscle tension to each segment. These *Isolation with Tension Exercises* should be practiced daily to gain the control needed for performing Mime convincingly.

1. Head isolation with tension

Stand in neutral position.

Tense the muscles behind your ears so that your ears are pulled back and up. Your face remains in neutral position.

Slowly tilt your head to the left. Keep your neck straight, but not stiff. Continue to keep your ear muscles tense throughout the isolation.

Bring your head up straight.

Tilt your head slowly to the right, feeling the pull of tension.

Return to neutral position.

Repeat.

Roll your head from the top of your spine in a clockwise motion, smoothly and evenly. Do not move your neck.

Return to neutral position.

Roll your head counterclockwise.

Return to neutral position.

Release the applied tension.

Relax. Maintain neutral position.

2. Neck isolation with tension

Stand in neutral position.

Push your lower jaw out as far as possible, with your teeth an inch apart.

Tense the corners of your mouth so that the throat musculature stiffens and the cords of your neck stand out.

Maintaining this tension, slowly move your head back until the edge of your skull touches the knot of vertebra that is between your shoulders in the middle of your back.

Return to neutral position.

Slowly move your head forward until your chin rests in the "V" at the base of your throat.

Return to neutral position.

Repeat and return to neutral position.

3. Shoulder isolation with tension

Stand in neutral position.

Pull your shoulders in, tightening the muscles around both collarbones.

Now, counterbalance by tightening the muscles in your back under the shoulderblades.

Roll your left shoulder in a downward motion. Do not move your neck, chest or other shoulder.

Return to neutral position.

Repeat the isolation slowly with the right shoulder, keeping your neck and chest still.

Stand in neutral position.

Roll *both* shoulders simultaneously in a circular motion: in, up, back, down, and front. Check your positioning in a mirror. Are your neck and chest relaxed?

Return to neutral position and relax.

4. Arm isolation with tension

Left arm isolation with tension. Standing in neutral position, extend left arm straight out from the side of your body.

Tense entire left arm so that the elbow feels "locked" in position.

Rotate the whole arm from the shoulder in a clockwise motion, making a circle the size of a basketball with your hand.

Return to neutral position.

Repeat the left arm isolation with a counterclockwise motion. Keep rechecking body position and breathing. Remember to relax all muscles not in use. Do not tighten your opposite shoulder. (This would cause tension across shoulder blades and defeat the purpose of neutral position.)

Left wrist isolation with tension. Raise your left arm, as in the previous exercise, keeping your right arm in neutral position.

Tense your left wrist, raising it straight up from your arm in a 90-degree angle, fingers pointing straight up, thumb stretched outward.

Keep arm tensed. The pressure applied to wrist should force more tension onto elbow area.

Rock wrist from side to side, maintaining tension in the wrist.

Repeat.

Left finger isolation with tension. With left arm extended, stretch fingers as far apart as possible.

Slowly tense the fingers and the thumb of your left hand into claw position.

Move your fingers and thumb in this position, until you feel the strong resistance to the pull from the opposing muscles.

Repeat.

Relax fingers, elbow, and then arm, slowly.

Return to neutral position.

Perform *arm isolation with tension* sequence with right arm, keeping left arm in neutral position.

5. Chest isolation with tension

Stand in neutral position. Place hands on hips.

Apply tension to muscles over breastbone.

Move chest area only—to the right, then to the left.

Repeat. Only the rib cage should be moving.

Draw your chest area in, then move it to the front, keeping constant tension. You should feel the pull in your breast and under your rib cage.

Repeat until mastered.

Return to neutral position.

6. Pelvis isolation with tension

Stand in neutral position.

Apply tension by tucking the buttocks in and under tightly.

Extend both arms out to the sides.
Rotate your pelvis clockwise.
Repeat.
Return to neutral position.

7. Leg isolation with tension

Stand in neutral position.

Extend your left leg to the left and bend your knee so that the calf and foot are extended downward.

Draw your foot up and out to the side so that your toes are pointing left. This will prevent leg cramps.

Apply tension to the entire leg. Feel the hard muscle in the back of your thigh and the calf.

Rotate leg slowly clockwise from the knee down, drawing a circle the size of a baseball.

Rotate counterclockwise.

Repeat the *Leg isolation with tension* sequence with your right leg.

Return to neutral position.

The following isolation is essential for mastery of the Mime Walk. Therefore, you must practice it repeatedly until you can perform this exercise correctly and automatically.

8. Foot isolation with tension

Stand in neutral position.

As you lift your left heel, press the ball and toes of your foot against the floor.

Feel the tension in the arch of your foot. There should be no tension in the upper leg or calf, just in the foot.

Roll foot back onto the heel, maintaining the tension.

Continue routine of heel, ball, toe, and the reverse—toe, ball, then heel.

9. Face isolation with tension

Perform the original *face isolation*. The face isolation sequence is the only exercise that, except for the jaw, does not involve the movement of bones. Instead, face isolation involves the fixed muscles of the face and their movement on the surface of the skull, so by their very nature, these exercises are already tension exercises. They are repeated here for your convenience.

Lip isolation with tension. While maintaining a relaxed neutral position, push your chin out from your face and turn under your lower lip. From that position, slowly move lip up and down several times. Keep chin still and the rest of your face relaxed.

Return to neutral position.

With your lips closed, tense corners of your mouth, as in a tight smile.

Move corners of your mouth up and down. You should feel the muscles in the corners of your upper lip working as you do this isolation. Feel the muscle under your chin.

In this same position, pull the tension in the lips from one side to the other repeatedly. Is the action free and smooth and uncomplicated by eyebrow motion? Remember, move only your lips.

Nose isolation with tension. From neutral position, concentrate on isolating your nose from the rest of your face. To perform this isolation, use the upper lip muscles. To begin, push your upper lip muscles up, as in a "sniff" position, crinkling the skin on your nose.

Repeat and return to neutral position.

Eye isolation. In neutral position, move your eyes from side to side.

Move both eyes in an up-and-down pattern.

Rotate eyes clockwise and then counterclockwise. Repeat, and return to neutral position.

Eyelid isolation with tension. Starting in a neutral position, slowly slide your upper eyelids downward until they are completely closed.
Repeat, and return to neutral position.

Eyebrow isolation with tension. In neutral position, isolate your eyebrows by moving muscles above and below eyebrows up and down. Keep your mouth still and relaxed.
Work each eyebrow individually.
Repeat and return to neutral position.

Full-face isolation with tension. In neutral position, drop your lower jaw and raise your eyebrows.
Stretch your face as far as possible, keeping lip and cheek muscles relaxed.

Repeat. Remember to use diaphragmatic breathing throughout this and all previous sequences.
Return to neutral position.
After completion of all Isolation Exercises with Tension, shake out and relax.

UNIT 3

Body Positions and Motion Exercises

Body Positions and Motion Exercises

STATIONARY ILLUSIONS

The mime must be able to produce in an audience a "willing suspension of disbelief." The viewers must actually feel they are seeing something that is not there; but they will "believe" only if the illusions are exact and well rehearsed.

To acquire the skill needed to perform convincing illusions, you must first have mastered diaphragmatic breathing and learned to control the various parts of your body through the Isolation Exercises with Tension of Unit 2.

In Unit 3, you will learn to incorporate the movements of separate parts of the body into "whole body patterns," thus creating an orchestrated movement that makes the illusion. Although these movements have actually been achieved by concentrated, persistent work and hours of rehearsal, they must appear spontaneous.

Remember: There is little room for error when creating illusions. Sloppy movements make unclear illusions, confusing onlookers and causing them to lose interest in the Mime performance.

Two typical examples of stationary illusions are the Statue and the Mannikin. Both are "frozen" poses for the onlooker to admire and enjoy. In performing the Mannikin, the mime tries to duplicate the appearance of a store window mannikin. This may be done in a store window, among department store "dummies," or any place where a shopper might least expect to find a live person.

The Statue can be performed anywhere, and the mime may use any unusual (but comfortable!) position to arouse the curiosity of passersby. The Statue is the more "obvious" of the two poses, and the street mime can use it to take a break between performing other illusions.

Here are some exercises that will help you perfect this technique of stationary body tension. Work in front of a full-length mirror.

Begin by holding a real egg in one hand. Feel its texture and weight. Look at the positioning of your hand and fingers. Are you using all of your fingers to hold it, or just the three fingers and thumb? The thumb and index only? Are you using your palm to support the egg at all?

How, "hold" an imaginary egg. Of course, there is nothing there, but you should be able to "feel" its weight and texture as you felt the weight and texture of the real egg, and you can show this by tensing your hand and wrist slightly. Bend your fingers slightly downward toward your palm, thumb pointing toward the index finger, thus showing the size of the egg.

As you hold the imaginary egg, study your body in the mirror, from top to bottom. Remember—this is a whole-body exercise! What attitude does your body posture convey to an onlooker? When in doubt, use the

Neutral Position for the parts of the body not directly involved in creating the illusion. All parts of the body should be working toward the illusion, or be in a neutral stance. You can improve the illusion of the egg by holding the "egg" out from your body, but away from your face. Through facial expressions, convey some emotion, such as curiosity or doubt about the egg.

This exercise should simply convey to the onlooker that you are holding a small, light object, nothing else. Any other hints or information the audience receives should come only from the title card used to announce the show.

Now, pick up a real bowling ball, and as you do, look in the mirror at all parts of your body: include feet, legs, pelvis, chest, arms, neck, head and face in your inventory. Study the amount of tension in the various parts of your body as you hold the ball. Where does your body hurt? In the shoulders? The upper arms? The parts of your body that feel pain while you are holding the real bowling ball are the parts you must tense to create the illusion of holding a bowling ball. Observe your hand positions—the thumb and two fingers of one hand are inserted into the three holes in the ball, and the other hand supports its weight.

Set the real bowling ball down, and pick up the imaginary ball. Don't forget the familiar thumb and two-finger position, which will help make the illusion believable and can be strengthened by tensing the lower hand more than the hand which balances the ball. Don't exaggerate the stress, however, and don't block your face with the ball.

Alternate holding the real and imaginary bowling balls—looking in the mirror all the time—until you see that you have achieved a semblance of the real thing.

BASIC BODY POSITIONS

Most of the illusions used in Mime are moving illusions. It is hard to depict something unless some action is associated with it. We can't tell that a mime is holding a flower unless he first reaches down, picks it, and smells it.

A moving illusion is not an exact duplication of a real-life action, however. The manner in which you pick an apple in an orchard is different from the way you would pick an apple on stage. Each movement that the mime makes, no matter how small or subtle, must be conscious and controlled, and slightly exaggerated to highlight and help define the action.

To make convincing moving illusions, you must first learn the *Five Basic Body Positions*, then practice the fundamental movements of Mime in the *Motion Exercises*.

FIRST POSITION, ARMS

FIRST POSITION, FEET

Five Basic Body Positions.

Learn these basic positions thoroughly. After mastering each position, work to move smoothly in sequence from first through fifth position. (Some people are unable to achieve an *exact* first or fifth position because of hyperextension of the legs, or other physical reasons. Understanding the positions is much more important than exact positioning.)

First Position

Stand in neutral position.

Hold your arms in front of your diaphragm, as if holding a beach ball.

Turn your feet 45 degrees out, heels slightly apart.

46

Second Position

    Stand in neutral position.

    Move arms out to the side with elbows slightly bent.

    Turn wrists in slightly.

    Stand with legs in an "A" shape, heels two feet apart. Toes should point out to left and right.

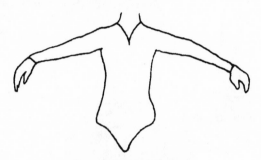

SECOND POSITION, ARMS

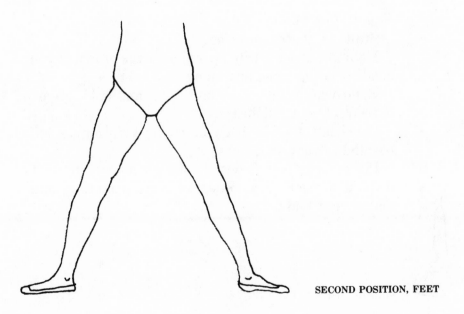

SECOND POSITION, FEET

Third Position

Stand in neutral position.

Lift your right arms above your head.

Bend your elbow slightly and turn your wrist in.

Extend your left arm straight out to the side.

Place right foot in front of left instep.

Point left toes left, heel right.

Place right heel in the arch of your left foot, toes pointed 45 degrees from the center line of your body.

THIRD POSITION, FEET

THIRD POSITION, ARMS

Fourth Position

Stand in neutral position.

Hold left arm slightly up and over the crown of your head, bending wrist and elbow.

Bend your right elbow and wrist and hold forearm in front of your diaphragm.

Place left foot in back of right, pointing to left, parallel to your shoulders.

Place right foot forward, about one foot from its neutral position, at a 45-degree angle from the center line of your body.

FOURTH POSITION, ARMS

FOURTH POSITION, FEET

48

Fifth Position

Stand in neutral position.

Hold arms at waist height, elbows slightly bowed, with fingertips close together.

FIFTH POSITION, ARMS

FIFTH POSITION, FEET

Place left foot close to back of right foot. Keep legs straight.

Point left toes left.

Point right toes right.

Feet should be parallel, with right foot in front. Right toe should be close to left heel. Left toe should be close to right heel.

MOTION EXERCISES

These exercises, which are just basic physical movements, will help the mime develop style and control.

Keep the motion energetic, simple, and clean. Breathe regularly throughout each step.

1. *Bend*

With feet in first position, place hands on hips, and slowly bend the knees outward, keeping your body in neutral position. Bend until you feel the pull at the back of your ankle and calf. Return to the beginning position.

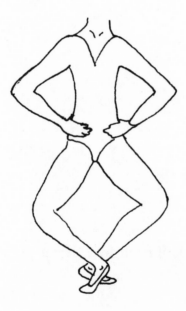

Repeat the bend exercise, progressing through all five basic body positions.

Return to neutral position.

2. *Forward Tilt*

With your feet in first position, lean forward without bending waist or knees. Keeping your feet flat on the floor, lean forward as far as possible.

Repeat. Try to lean farther forward with each repeat.

3. *Back Tilt*

With your feet in first position, arms extended straight out to the side of your body, imagine that a weight is pulling you back from the center of your body. Lean back as far as possible without moving your feet or arms.

Return to first position.

Repeat. Go back a bit farther each time.

Return to neutral position.

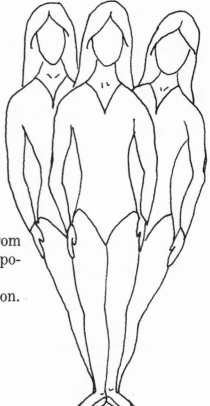

4. *Side Tilt*

Stand in neutral position.

From the midsection of your body, bend slowly from side to side, tilting farther each time. The foot opposite the tilt should not leave the ground.

Keep relaxed. Breathe in rhythm with the motion. Go a bit farther to each side each time.

Return to neutral position.

SIDE TILT

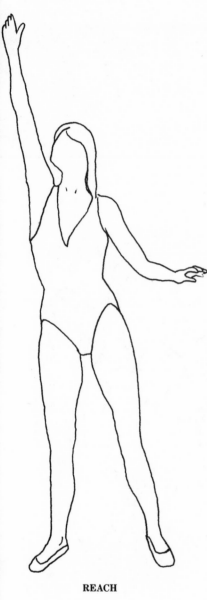

5. *Reach*

Stand in neutral position.

Extend your left arm straight up above your head, pulling your entire body up with it. Follow the movement of the extended arm with your eyes.

6. *Bending to Pick Up*

A mime must bend to pick something up in such a way that will be clearly seen and understood by everyone in the audience. It cannot be done in the spontaneous and offhand way a non-mime would bend over to pick something up off the street.

Begin with your feet in fourth position, arms in neutral position.

Bend from the knees, keeping the upper portion of your body in a slight forward tilt.

Extend your right arm forward, while extending the left arm out from the shoulder and slightly upward. Pick up an imaginary object while keeping your face and chin visible to the audience.

Return to neutral position.

REACH

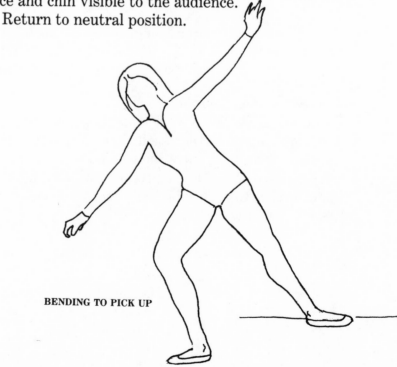

BENDING TO PICK UP

UNIT 4

Moving Illusions

Moving Illusions

Now that you have mastered the Five Basic Body Positions and the Motion Exercises, you are ready to create true Mime illusions: the *Moving Illusions*. In moving illusions, your whole body is involved, is focused on the illusion. Each movement must shift smoothly into the next, if the audience is to continue to believe that something is happening with nothing.

Illusions

First, visualize the illusion, then the movement needed to produce it. You must convince yourself of the "reality" of the object you are creating before others will believe it.

Flower. Picture a flower. Decide what kind of flower it is, what relationship its size has to your body, how tall it is, where its leaves are, if it has thorns, and where the bud begins and ends. You must "see" this flower before you can begin the necessary movements for the illusion.

Once you have visualized the flower, stand with your legs in the fourth position.

Bend slowly from the knees, pushing your chest slightly forward.

Reach out to the flower, sweeping your right hand out from your body.

With your right hand out as in the Wrist Isolation with Tension Exercise, roll your hand in. . .

Tilt hand down. . .

Push wrist up. . .

Close your index finger and thumb around the stem.

Pluck the stem with a pinching motion, quickly pushing your wrist down and fingers up. Keep your face turned somewhat toward the audience.

Focusing on the flower, raise your body in the same fashion as you lowered it.

Lift the flower to smell it. Keep your hand and extended fingers just below chin level and push your chin out as you smell the flower. Don't pick a flower of one length and have it appear longer or shorter when you smell it.

What to do with your flower

a. *Put it in your hair:* Move your right hand, which holds the imaginary flower, in front of your face as you turn your head right. Your chin should be in line with the "V" of your bent elbow. Stick the flower in your hair with a clean, precise wrist action.

b. *Put it in your lapel:* With a downward thrust, insert the flower into the "buttonhole" of your lapel.

c. *Throw it away:* With a flick of the wrist, toss the flower away from your body, off to one side. Follow the movement of the flower with your eyes.

Give it to someone in the audience (only in Street Mime): Present the flower to the closest smiling person, or put it in someone else's hair.

Every illusion must have a definite beginning and end. An effective mime realizes that each sequence must be clearly introduced and clearly concluded, leaving no doubt in the mind of onlookers.

Balloon. Reach into your imaginary pocket with your right hand, thumb behind the fingers. Emphasize the action by raising your right hip and bending your knee. Keep left leg straight, so that the ball of your left foot now supports your body weight.

As you pull the "deflated balloon" out of your pocket with your right hand, focus your attention on it. Return to regular standing position.

Make motion of shaking balloon in front of you, below your chin, being careful not to obstruct your face.

Take hold of the other end of the balloon with your left hand.

Stretch the balloon by using the arm tension exercise for both arms to create the illusion of elastic resistance. Stretch it several times, then hold the balloon in your left hand.

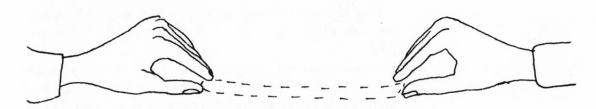

Envision the deflated balloon in your left hand, turn your body slightly to the right and place the balloon opening in your mouth. Using your index finger and thumb to squeeze the opening, curl other fingers around opening and position it about one inch from your mouth.

Open your mouth and inhale by raising your chest, bending back slightly to make the illusion visible to the audience. Make no sound.

Grasp the end of the balloon with your lips (using lip isolation) and force the air into your cheeks, puffing them out.

With a thrusting motion, appear to force air from the cheeks into the balloon.

Show the balloon expanding by cupping your right hand in front of your chin. Move the hand and arm out by curving your elbow as in the first position arm movement. Tension should be visible only in the fingers, neck and face.

After this balloon–blowing sequence, return your right arm to your side. Keep holding the balloon opening with your left hand.

Pull the end of the balloon away from your mouth (as you exhale). Indicate this by releasing the tension in your neck and face. Make no exhalation noise.

Reach into your imaginary pocket with your right hand and pull out an imaginary string.

Shake the string as you slowly draw it up to the balloon.

Quickly wind string around end of balloon by making a small circular motion. Balloon remains in the left hand.

Holding string in right hand, release balloon with left hand and follow it with your eyes and face. Remember that the ballon can only float as high as the string is long.

Reach up and pat the balloon with your left hand.

What to do with the balloon

a. *Release it:* Watch it float away.

b. *Have it burst:* With an astonished expression on your face, show shock at the "pop" sound.

c. *Tie it* on the wrist of someone near you, real or imaginary, and give balloon a pat as you move away.

Wall

The illusion of the wall is an important Mime convention. The wall must seem convincingly real. The audience will believe your illusion only if the wall is "solid."

Visualize a wall. Decide how high and how long it is, what its texture is, and if it will have a door or window in it.

When the image is set in your mind, begin the action.

Stand in neutral position.

Raise the top of your right wrist to chest level, hand in a limp position. Hold elbow at waist level.

Bend wrist of your right hand upward so palm is facing audience. Your hand is now shoulder high but slightly to the left of your shoulder. Fingers, spread apart, should extend upward from palm, not bent back or curved forward.

Keep your hand relaxed with just enough tension to keep the palm straight up.

Repeat same procedure with your left hand. Position palm to left side of your body. Focus on the "wall." This is the *Wall Position*.

Try to keep all elements of your body action uncovered and visible to the audience. Remember: your feet must not inadvertently intrude into the plane of wall. Keep your hands in front of the line of your toes.

With both hands in correct wall position, you may begin to move along wall, indicating its length and height to your audience.

Begin by moving your chest and shoulders to the right, keeping your hands in stationary position.

Lift wrist of right hand from the wall and roll your fingers in a circular movement into the new wall position to the right of your right shoulder.

WALL POSITIONS ⟶

60

Repeat with your left hand, arriving at new wall position to the right of the left shoulder.

Take one or two steps to the right, making sure you do not step into the wall. Your fingers should be below chin level; push your neck forward as if peeking over your right hand.

Repeat this pattern—chest move, right hand move, left hand move, step; chest move, right hand move, left hand move, step—until it becomes natural.

This illusion may be varied by moving left hand first.

To show height of wall, start in the wall position.

Release right hand by drawing your wrist back toward your throat, holding elbow stationary, and fingers now extended toward the audience.

Raise right hand, still bent, twelve inches above your shoulder. This action will carry your elbow along.

Place your hand at new height, palm out, onto plane of the wall. Check to see that both hands are on the same wall plane.

Repeat sequence with your left hand.

Lower hands in same fashion.

Explore walls of various heights, lengths, and curvatures. Feel your way around a tall tower. Imagine yourself trapped in a small room.

Insert a door. Keep your body in neutral position.

"Walk" your right and left hand up and down the wall to indicate the door's height.

Walk your hands down into the wall position. Reach for doorknob by taking your right hand off door and tensing your fingers in a semicircle, fingers on one side thumb rounded on the other. Keep your left hand pressed against door.

Twist right wrist to open the door, while simultaneously rolling your right shoulder forward.

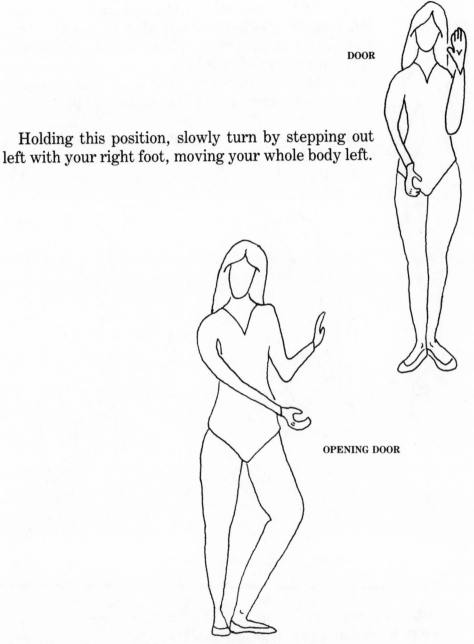

DOOR

Holding this position, slowly turn by stepping out left with your right foot, moving your whole body left.

OPENING DOOR

Release both hands, dropping them to the sides of your body. Adjust entire body to face forward.

Insert a window. Start in the wall position. Keeping left hand in this position (on what is now the "window"), turn palm of your right hand upward and bring it toward center of your body.

Repeat using left hand. Both hands should now be next to each other, palms flat and facing up.

Give a quick push up, about two inches, and bending at your knees, quickly turn both hands outward, still flat. This is the position used to push window rest of the way up.

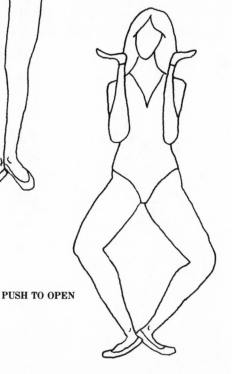

PUSH TO OPEN

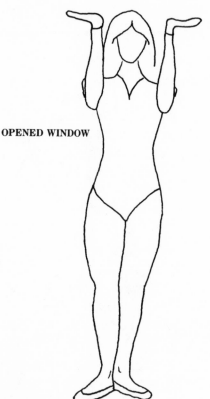

OPENED WINDOW

Push imaginary window up until the flat hands are above your head and your legs are straight.
Release hands and relax your body.
Reach through window to shake someone's hand.

Push-Pull. To create the related illusions of pushing and pulling, a mime must combine various tensions, motion exercises, and the technique of depicting heavy weight by showing tension (remember the bowling ball?).

All objects have weight. To show this convincingly in Mime, the resistance must be exaggerated. To move a heavy object in Mime, exaggerated force must be shown by performing exaggerated and dramatized tensions, whether fighting "gravity" or "inertia." But don't overdo it. A box is lighter than a heavy safe!

Push. When pushing an "object," try to make it appear to be twice its real weight. Pretend to push a crate.

In neutral position, face stage left.

Visualize a heavy crate.

Place your hands in wall position, thus showing your audience the crate's edge.

Inhale dramatically. Make no noise while inhaling.

Lean forward and turn your head to side, to face audience.

Show tension in your face, neck, shoulders, chest, arms, wrists, and hands.

Appear to push by forcing your arms to move from their bent position to a new position two or three inches forward.

At the same time, move your body laboriously by stepping forward with the left foot.

Apply tension to the left leg and force your knee to bend, and rolling your foot up onto the toes.

Push forcefully from the toe and knee area to the new position and shift body weight onto your right leg, thus repeating the sequence.

Repeat the illusion while moving offstage.

TUG-OF-WAR

Pull. Play Mime Tug-of-War. In this game, a mime with one foot planted in front of the other pulls a rope, and strains at one end of it.

Facing your audience, stand with your feet in second position.

Extend your left arm to the side. Extend your right arm, bent at the elbow, left, across your body.

Hollow out your hands as if holding a rope. Never allow your hands to close completely.

Tilt your body left by bending your right knee. This is your beginning position.

POSITION A, TUG-OF-WAR

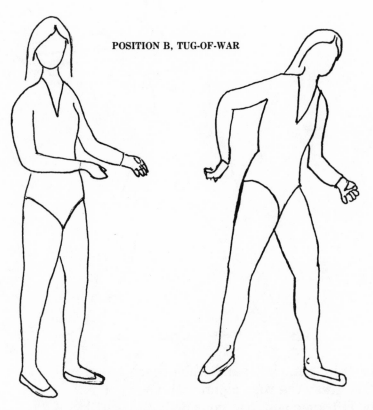

POSITION B, TUG-OF-WAR

Now, "pull" on the imaginary rope. To do this, straighten your upper body, at the same time moving your arms slightly to the right of your body's center. This is Position B.

Drop the imaginary rope from your right hand, then reach in front of your left hand and grasp the rope again with the right. Your arms should be crossed. You are now in Position C.

POSITION C, TUG-OF-WAR

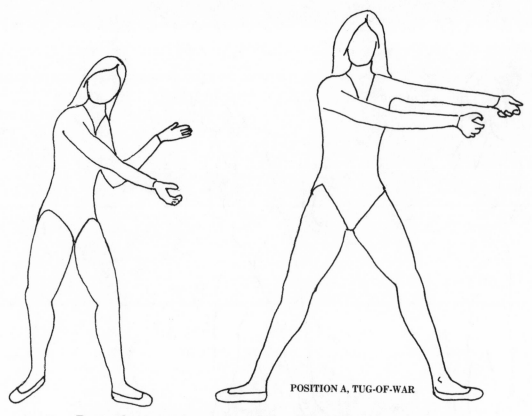

POSITION A, TUG-OF-WAR

Drop the rope from your left hand, then reach behind the right and grasp the rope again with your left
hand. Bend your left knee and lean your body toward
your hands. You are now in Position A.

Repeat Positions A, B, and C to create a smooth,
tugging motion.

Portray losing the Tug-of-War. Lunge forward in
the direction of the tug, in this case to the right, by
thrusting your body into a fall, thus showing defeat.

Portray winning. Keep the pull (from Position B)
strong, and slowly move backwards. The more you
pull back, the more you should shift your body left, as
indicated in Position B. Portray winning by decisively
and triumphantly dragging the "opponent" offstage.
As you move backwards, continue to show the strain
of pulling, but add the new facial element of delight in
winning.

Repeat the illusion while moving offstage.

Mime Walks

The illusion of the Mime Walk in both its variations is actually a Moving Exercise performed in one spot. It requires practice to become smooth and convincing.

Remember to use diaphragmatic breathing.

Profile Walk
Beginning stance
Face stage left.

Bend left arm at the elbow, holding forearm parallel to floor.

Tilt wrist slightly down.

Hold right arm almost straight down, slightly bent at elbow, extending back no more than three inches behind you.

Bend right leg at the knee.

Hold heel of right foot off the floor, ball and toe touching the floor.

Keep left leg straight, supporting weight of body.

Movement one
Step (do not slide) right heel forward one step. Keep all other body positions the same. Keep your right toes two inches off the floor.

Movement two
Slide the right heel backwards, causing the ball and toe of right foot to slide along with the heel into a resting or neutral position.

Simultaneously, lift left foot onto its ball and toe by bending your knee, and move arms so that your right arm is now bent forward, and your left arm, slightly bent at the elbow, moves behind your body two to three inches. Your right leg now supports the body weight.

PROFILE WALK

Movement three

Place left heel one step in front of its neutral position, but keep toes two inches off the floor.

Movement four

Slide left heel backwards into neutral position.

Simultaneously lift right foot onto the ball and toe by bending your right knee.

At the same time, move left arm so that it is now bent forward, forearm parallel to the floor; and move right arm, slightly bent at the elbow, two to three inches behind body.

Repeat the entire sequence until the Profile Walk is comfortable and realistic. Do not make it harder than it is!

Frontal Walk

Perform the Frontal Walk facing the audience. A funny or unique style of walk (such as the Charlie Chaplin walk) will be more obvious to the audience from this angle.

Repeat the technique you have learned in the Profile Walk, but point the feet more sharply outward. Remember to hold your head up, so that your face is visible to the audience.

Using these two basic styles of walks, the mime can create many different angles of action and movement.

FRONTAL WALK

Climbs

There are three essential climb illusions: the Staircase Climb, the Rope Climb, and the Ladder Climb. To master these climbs, you must (a) constantly and accurately visualize the support object (staircase, rope, or ladder), and (b) constantly show varying degrees of strain as you climb.

Remember: The illusion of your body passing the support object must always be kept in mind. This support must always appear "solid" to the audience.

The force of the strain in climbs, as in other illusions, is once again shown convincingly by tensing the appropriate muscles.

Breathing (silent!) must be made visible to the audience to make the action believable. Breathing and panting in combination with the movements of these climbs make the illusions look real.

Staircase Climb—Up
Beginning stance

Focus eyes upward.

Face stage left in neutral position.

Tilt chest (not shoulders) slightly forward.

Hold right arm out in front of you, three inches above shoulder height (as if holding a bannister rail), elbow slightly bent.

Place fingers with thumb opposite middle finger, so that your hand is cupped around a space the size of a bannister railing.

Movement one

With right side to audience, slide right foot forward three or four inches and roll onto ball of foot.

At the same time, move right arm back to body by bending elbow. Apply pulling tension to show the strain of your arm pulling on the rail as you climb upstairs.

STAIRCASE CLIMB

Movement two (to be performed simultaneously with movement one)

Slide right foot back from ball onto heel, while lifting left foot to its ball, pushing knee forward.

With right hand, "release" rail and reach up on a diagonal to grasp a new "handhold."

Continue movements one and two until you have reached the top of the stairs.

Staircase Climb—Down

Face stage right with left hand on rail.

Repeat the same sequence of movements as in the *Staircase—Up*, except that the focus of the movement is downward and the sides of your body are reversed—*left* arm is *lowered, left* hand grasps rail at hip level. Keep your face visible to the audience without losing the illusion created by the downward tilt of your head.

Rope Climb—Up

Beginning stance

Stand in neutral position.

Envision the rope three feet in front of you. Notice its texture, width, and length.

Walk three feet toward the audience and stop, facing forward.

Stand with feet in third position, arms down at your sides, body relaxed.

Reach up with right hand and "grab" rope, with exaggerated motion.

Movement one

Perform all action four to five inches in front of your body. Raise left arm and grab rope above your right hand. Keep your arms extended over your head.

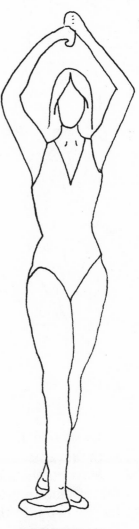

ROPE CLIMB

Movement two
With tension and stress applied to forearms, shoulder, chest area, and face, pull hands down to just below chin, while moving elbows out to the sides, and up almost to shoulder level.

ROPE CLIMB

Movement three (to be performed simultaneously with movement two)
Move knees apart, by rolling feet up onto balls of feet. Come to rest on balls and toes of feet. Roll feet back down into third position, as arms are moving to their position in movement two.

Repeat movements one, two, and three in this order:

> Right hand grab,
> Left hand grab,
> Roll up,
> Tug,
> Roll down, etc.

Climb variations. While rolling up onto toes, keep right leg in bent position, while letting the other leg fly out—as if it were hard to hang on!

Rope Climb—Down

Use the same sequence as *Rope Climb—Up,* but now all motions should take place above your head. Focus down and out to the audience. Reverse *Rope Climb—Up* sequence. Move rapidly.

Ladder Climb—Up

To perform the classic Ladder Climb, you do not put your hands on imaginary crossbars. Instead, you seem to pull yourself up with the side rails, so that your face remains unobstructed in both frontal and side views.

Beginning stance

Stand in neutral position.

Raise both forearms straight up, in a vertical position. Elbows and shoulders remain in neutral position.

Bend wrists outward, palms facing each other.

Grasp the side rails of "ladder" four inches in front of you.

Fix this hand grip in your mind. Fix ladder width in your mind. Fix crossbar spacing in your mind. If you don't, you may inadvertently portray climbing a rubber ladder!

Movement one

Use the same stepping motion as in the *Staircase Climb—Up*, except that your feet must come *straight down* again (no sliding back into position).

With left foot, step up with the ball, then toe, sequence.

Movement two

As foot is stepping, pull hands down to lower chest, giving the illusion of moving up. Your elbows must move outward so that your hands move downward in exact parallel position.

Movement three

With your left foot back in neutral position, extend right hand up to grasp a higher ladder side rail position. Follow with a higher left hand position.

Movement four

Repeat movement one with right foot.

Repeat movement sequence till you reach top of ladder. Check for accurate placement of hands. Remember to breathe from the diaphragm.

ILLUSIONS WITH REACTIONS

After gaining a certain physical control and learning some basic moving illusions, the mime must set these illusions within an emotional context, or any performance will remain mere physical mimicry. If a mime doesn't show his reactions to his illusions, the audience won't, either. There must be a reason for every movement. A strictly physical display of illusions carries no thread of meaning to engage the audience's attention. A person in whiteface simply climbing an invisible staircase will not hold the audience's attention for long. The mime must have an "opinion" about every action in order to create a believable illusion.

The emotional reactions that can be revealed for the

various moving illusions are almost unlimited. The simple action of picking a flower can convey a feeling of joy or sorrow, curiosity, surprise, tenderness, or even cold aloofness.

Repeat the flower illusion, each time showing a different one of these emotions.

Perform the balloon illusion expressing surprise, exhaustion, anger, or excitement. Combine two emotions. Show various emotions in performing different parts of the illusion: inflating the balloon, tying the end, giving the balloon away, or having it burst.

Perform the wall illusion. Plot a progression of emotions to tell a story. Show excitement building with each step as you peer around, stop suddenly as you hear a strange sound, peek cautiously over the wall as you try to discover the source of the noise.

Develop the push-pull illusion by affecting attitudes of stress, determination, energy, extreme fatigue, or laziness.

In the walk illusion, show exhaustion. Be happy. Be sad. Be carefree. Fight a strong wind that is pushing at your front or back. Stop from time to time to see something close or far away.

In all three of the climb illusions, add a touch of boredom, danger, exhaustion, or the excitement of discovery.

IMPROVISATION EXERCISES

A good way to develop on-the-spot creativity is to combine an illusion with a random emotion.

To come up with a spontaneous idea, simply imagine yourself in a particular situation and act accordingly.

Example: Use the *Staircase Climb—Up* combined with the emotion fear. Create a situation that gives you a *reason* to react to danger. The steps and railing could be rickety and rotted. Someone could be holding you at gunpoint. You could be afraid of heights. Imagine yourself combining all of these in the dark.

A few words of basic acting advice: Experienced actors know that it is possible to guide an audience to feel an emotion by choosing one of three focal points.

Up. If you choose a focal point above the level of your head, you will convey a visual picture of hope, fantasy, or any other essentially positive emotion.

Across. When you focus the attention of the audience at eye level, you are communicating reality. Focusing at this level can be a very intense experience, and should therefore be used selectively and only for short periods of time.

Down. Whether you are conveying depression, befuddlement, fear, sorrow, or any other "negative" emotion, focus your eyes down. Your whole body should curve inward and down. Depending on the intensity of the emotion, roll shoulders in, and push chest down. Cast head and eyes down, as well, but don't hide your face from the audience.

Remember: These three level techniques are just starting points for emotional expression. Specific emotions at each level are drawn and refined through an expressive face and expressive hands, and convincing body posture.

Emotional reactions justify Mime action and lay the groundwork for further characterization and plot.

UNIT 5

Characterization and Character

Characterization and Character

CHARACTERIZATION is the process of creating the role (the character) required by the plot or story and inventing the physical Mime moves to express it. The mime's job is to analyze the elements of the character (personality, emotions, attitudes, etc.) and to work out the sequence of physical motions (mannerisms, facial expressions, and any other subtle gestures) that can convincingly portray it.

The character is the most important aspect of Mime. Since Mime does not use the spoken language, it cannot have a complicated plot. In fact, a mime's portrayal of a character can color the whole plot and even change the plot's meaning through varying actions, gestures, and facial expressions.

Actors play the role Hamlet in many different ways. The words and stage directions for the role have remained unchanged for over four hundred years, but each actor, through his interpretaton of Hamlet's personality and character and by using his own gestures, mannerisms and other visual signals, brings a unique emphasis to the story. Hamlet has been played as a vengeful prince, a vacillating and unsure young man swept along by events, and even as depressed and world-weary. This is how a unique interpretation of a character can emerge from the same role.

How Is Character Used?

In Mime characterization, even the simplest action, such as picking a "flower," requires some sort of personality backdrop (if only a bright smile), or the mime's action remains at an exercise level—flat and unfeeling.

For street Mime, the character may be simple. In the "mini" shows of street Mime, there is little time to develop character. The mime spends most of his time "playing with people" and uses Mime technique for making illusions of "objects" (i.e. "balloons," "flowers," etc.) to interact with the changing audience.

A good basic character for street Mime is one who is seen by the onlookers as honest, sincere, funny, clever, and empathic—a friendly person, though a stranger. People will quickly warm up to this character, thus making the mime's job easier.

For stage Mime, a full and more complicated development of character is needed. To hold an audience's attention and interest with at least one fifteen-minute pantomime, more than a few casual motions are required. For stage performance, the mime must analyze the character to be portrayed and then choose a set of physical actions that will show the character's appearance, personality, character, and intent. These actions must reveal both the physical (outer) appearance and the psychological (inner) state.

Performance Character

Many mimes develop a unique performance character. This "personal" character often serves as a familiar protagonist in many of a mime's performances, and may even be thought of as his alterego.

Repeated use of his own, special character enables the performer to play three characters simultaneously!

1. *The performer as a mime.* The performer is, first and foremost, a mime. The art form of Mime has definite rules and conventions of performance. A person who takes on the character of a mime must speak with his body and tell a story by moving in predetermined ways. This is done by performing rehearsed physical sequences. The mime's style may reflect years of dance training and athletic or gymnastic experience, but the personality and character must be essentially neutral.

2. *The mime as a performance character.* To the basic Mime form, a performer may add a personal touch or "trademark" to create a performance character. A physical trademark, such as a cocked hat, indicates a special attitude toward life and helps create an identity for a specific mime. In this way, the mime may develop a following: Audiences recognize the "trademark" and anticipate the mime's unique performance character. This is a stylistic touch only—not a change of the neutral Mime role.

3. *The performance character in different roles.* The performance character may play different roles as diverse as babysitter or saxophone player, but always within the framework of his special character.

For example: World-famous teacher and Mime performer Marcel Marceau steps on stage and becomes:

A mime: Marcel Marceau has over his lifetime developed a system of techniques and attitudes based on the traditional school of French Mime. He teaches and displays demanding standards of physical performance.

A performance character: Marceau has created the famous character, "Mr. Bip." Known the world over, Mr. Bip wears a flower in his top hat and is ever the whimsical realist.

A performance character in different roles: Mr. Bip finds himself in many different roles. He may be cast in the role of an artist in one pantomime, a lion tamer in another. However, his reactions, even if unexpected or far-fetched, fall within the character possibilities of Mr. Bip.

With an understanding of your basic character, as a mime you can go on to develop the continuing personality of your performance character in the different pantomimes. Make your performance character's trademark or symbol obvious and simple, so that you can take on the varied roles and situations required in the different pantomimes, and yet be recognizable to the audience. However, it isn't necessary for you always to perform Mime as your performance character.

How to develop a character

Before you construct the range of physical actions that will portray your character, you must decide what it is that you want to show. Study the role and list the good and bad characteristics of your character. What happens in the plot gives you the starting point. As you rework the list, try to add secondary characteristics that reflect other, less obvious aspects of your character: A king might be proud of his strong physique but embarrassed by his thinning hair, as a sign of aging. A miser who is normally timid and fearful might become agitated and grasping around money.

This list can be used later to develop the Mime gestures needed to create the specific emotions desired. This process of transforming the ideas into actual movements will be discussed in the Unit on *Rehearsal*.

You should understand the distinction between personality and character. Stated simply, *personality* is the "persona" or mask mimes wear in relating to other people or animals. A salesman portrays helpful friendliness to a customer. A matron gushes loving nonsense to her poodle.

Character is one's total personal background—his beliefs, feelings, and attitudes. A person may be patriotic or religious, honest or unscrupulous, or a combination of these, i.e. patriotic and religious. One person may consider himself honest, but gossip a lot. A despicable character may have a charming personality, as many villains have, in literature and in life.

Your Mime characterization should include a mix of personality (surface appearance and actions) and character (emotional background and beliefs).

With your list of character and personality attributes in hand, begin to look for physical motions that will show these inner states. And, as you analyze them, you may see other ways to present them.

Here are some basic *physical* characterizations to help you start:

1. *Age*. Age is an obvious physical aspect of a character. If the audience has a feeling for the character's age, they can better understand your actions.

An *aged person* can be presented in the following manner:

Start in neutral position.

Roll your backbone forward.

Roll your shoulders forward and up slightly to hollow out your chest area.

Thrust your neck and head forward from your shoulder, as in the Neck Isolation Exercise (no tension), to give a "squinting" appearance.

Without opening your mouth pull your jaw down, to give a drawn and aged look to your face.

Move slowly and maintain this position throughout the patomime. Emotions should be played with restraint. Age must be expressed with the whole body, not just your face or posture. A character is old "all over."

A *child* below the age of two is best played sitting or kneeling, and should have quick motions and rapidly changing moods—content one moment and screaming for food the next.

You play a screaming infant with your mouth wide open. To portray a crying child, keep your mouth closed or barely open and move your shoulders up and down together in a jerky fashion. For periods of one or two seconds, show that you are taking a deep breath. To do this, close your mouth part way and open your eyes as wide as possible. At the same time, stretch your upper body as far as you possibly can.

As a *child* two years or older, you should skip or run rather than walk. Your actions should be quick and not always coordinated. Fall down easily. Act as if you aren't always aware of where you are going. Keep in mind that young children do not always have their emotions under control, and therefore, their emotional reactions are somewhat unpredictable.

2. *Habits.* Habits are an easily identifiable part of most people's make-up. Everyone has habits: nail biting, fidgeting, pushing hair away from the face, and so on. You can add spice to a Mime characterization with these seemingly offhand movements.

3. *Emotional signatures*. While the habit of finger drumming usually indicates temporary impatience, wriggling your fingers and smirking may indicate a much deeper and more serious character trait like greed. Such an emotional signature is very different from a habit, though both are revealed by often unconscious physical movement.

A person cornered in a lie is characterized by evasive, darting eyes. A slothful character will set his body in slow motion. A belligerent person will place his whole body in an aggressive stance, rooted to the ground.

The challenge for you as a mime is to reflect these emotional signatures in body language and Mime movements and make them appear to be spontaneous.

4. *Physical conditions*. Physical conditions or traits can help define your overall characterization. The person you portray may be deaf, blind, very short, very tall, pregnant, lame, and so on. The audience's awareness of any particular physical trait helps them anticipate future actions that you will act out as part of your characterization.

When you portray a blind person, you should react to your environment in a tentative way, with your head tilted to the side to indicate that you are "looking" with your ear.

To characterize a very short person, you should look up most of the time, shake hands above the level of your shoulders, stand on tiptoe to see over things, and so on.

One way to characterize a very tall person is to stoop. Lower your head to get through a mime door, for instance.

Pregnant women can't bend from the waist and should be characterized that way.

The characterization of each of these physical conditions must always be maintained and reinforced throughout the story as you present it.

How to research and analyze physical movements

Where does the mime go to find and study personalities and characters he may want to use in his shows? The answer may be as simple as walking to the street corner or going to a shopping mall. Here at first hand are thousands of subjects we can imagine, if not actually see, in all kinds of situations. Choose a specific place where you can find the kind of people you have in mind for a characterization. At the outset you may or may not have a plot in mind. If you do, this can help direct your search; if not, what you see as you observe may give you ideas for story lines and characters.

Plot development (covered in Unit 6, *Playwriting*) does not necessarily have to precede characterization. Given the simple story lines used in Mime, it is often better to develop a character and then build a story around it.

Restaurants are good places to study people. (It may even be possible to interview a subject in certain circumstances.) Even more specific character possibilities may be found in such places as rock concerts, church services, bread lines, airports, lines waiting to go into movies, rest homes, nurseries, and army induction centers.

As you view people, try to determine if their physical actions are reflections of surface or of deeper feelings. For instance, the actions of TV game show contestants, watched by millions of viewers, are much different from those of subway riders, who, in the midst of noise and crowds and yet detached from their surroundings, may unexpectedly clench their hands or furrow their brows. These are actions you can learn from and build on.

Use your ingenuity to locate groups where you can observe real-world characters. Mime is a study of people.

Another place for character study is the entertainment world. Television, movies, and live theater offer dramatizations of real life, though a mime must screen out the language, camera angles, special technical effects, etc.

The television situation comedy show is a good example. This widely used format features a leading comedian who delivers the jokes and usually has the punch lines. As the joke progresses, try to disregard the audience's laughter and the camera work, and watch the character's body movements—the way his shoulders move up and down, his jaw falls open, or his neck thrusts forward. A mime must use all these "body language" techniques, but on a more exaggerated and conscious level.

Old silent movies and cartoons offer the best place to study *visual* action and facial expression without words. Here, camera close-ups and angles and other distracting framing devices are not as widely used, and there is no canned laughter or applause to coax the audience into the desired emotional response.

Cartoons are short on dialogue and long on the physical portrayal of character. Simple cartoon characters such as the Seven Dwarfs deliberately build their characters on physical appearance and gestures. There is no question who Bashful, Happy, and Grumpy are. We can see their characteristics in their actions and facial expressions. They show us with their faces, hands and postures.

Every cartoon rabbit's ears flop here and there to show us what is happening and what he is thinking at each moment: straight up means alert or fearful, one ear up and one down means relaxed or quizzical; both down means dejected or tired. These are the kinds of basic stereotypes useful to mimes.

In silent movies, such as one with Charlie Chaplin, we see the actor's characterization, as well as a story and often a "moral" or theme. Not only does Chaplin's every gesture, glance, and pose clearly tell us what is going on moment by moment at the surface, but his physical portrayal also constantly reflects his deeper character and thoughts. Along with a story, what we see in a Chaplin silent film is the silent expression of the full range of human emotions.

In these and other media, you should study the technique of other performers, whether actors or animators. Keep in mind the basic purpose of characterization research and analysis. How can you, the mime, use the mannerisms, gestures, and facial expressions of those performers to create your own characters and communicate them visually and in a convincing manner?

Putting it all together

So far you have been listing ideas and collecting information. Now you can begin to organize it all to build a character.

Here are three rules to help you sift through the many possibilities:

Three rules of creating a character

a. A character's outward appearance must be plausible. We know from our experience in life that certain types have attitudes and personality traits that may be predicted by their appearance. We expect a sloppy person with garish clothes to be loud and opinionated. We expect a neat, well-groomed person to be conscientious and deliberate.

b. The character must make sense within itself. A characterization must be internally coherent. Various motions must accurately express personality traits, and the emotions projected must fit the character. Also, all the character traits should have some relation to the story line. Unnecessary mannerisms and movements or gestures serve only to confuse the audience.

c. The Mime character is expressed by a combination of actions that convey both the outer appearance (personality, physique, dress) and the inner state (psychological make-up, hopes, dreams, emotions).

When you feel comfortable with your character's traits and your ability to express them physically, rewrite the list. This time list the movements in the order you will need to use them to build the characterization. If you have no plot in mind, this can be only a preliminary plan. If you have the plot in mind, build the character, taking the plot into account. Ask yourself, what should come first? What personality trait must be shown before the first action? What can be added later to flesh out the character as the story progresses? Start with little "loaded" movements. Brushing away a "fly" can start to reveal irritability or playfulness—whichever way the plot goes.

Finally, write a detailed plan of the physical actions. This is more than a pantomime script, which is only a general indication of what happens. This guide will help you initially learn the pantomime in the proper order and prevent you from leaving anything out. Once the *parts* and *sequence* of the characterization are memorized, you can discard this guide and rely on your general understanding and memory as you perform.

UNIT 6

Playwriting

Playwriting

A PANTOMIME is a dramatic form using expressive body movements, but no words, to convey a story and express the feelings and emotions of a character. It falls somewhere between a formal drama and pure improvisation. The "script" for a pantomime is actually a synopsis of the action and serves more as a general outline than as a step-by-step guide to movements.

Mimes have to create their own pantomime scripts, but this seeming limitation is actually an advantage. The mime, as playwright, knows best his own strengths and weaknesses, and as an actor, his likes and dislikes. By composing his own script, the mime knows the story line and its possibilities thoroughly. He has tailored it specifically for himself—a definite confidence booster in performance.

WRITING A PANTOMIME SCRIPT

A pantomime plot must be simple, and easy to follow. It should reflect the mime's mastery of the art, and not be too demanding for his skill level, but complex enough to be challenging and to hold the attention of his audience. If he is performing for a "special" audience—children, the deaf, the sick or disabled, or senior citizens, for example—he must prepare the script with his viewers in mind. Some audiences are "theater sophisticated," while others respond at a very elementary level.

Where to start

As a playwright, you must first find an idea that can be developed and adapted to pantomime. There are many sources for ideas.

1. List your Mime skills and illusions. Draw ideas from different combinations, but use the improvisation method described in Unit 4. Use only those skills you have mastered.

2. Listen to music (a symphony, instrumental record, but no singing): A favorite tune will often spark your imagination. (Music with words will restrict you to acting out the sentiment in the lyrics of a song.)

3. Think of the mood evoked by one of your favorite poems.

4. Think of your experiences and memories, and make a list of nouns,—fire, childhood, subway, baseball, crowds, dances, and others that trigger emotional responses in you, sad or happy—and carry emotional "freight." Everyone has memories that, when recalled, still bring pain or pleasure, melancholy or happiness, surprise, bewilderment, or fear.

5. Old fables or children's stories that are familiar to most people offer an excellent starting place for a beginning mime. The *Genie in the Lantern* is a good

example. (The mime finds a lantern, rubs it, and a genie emerges who gives him three wishes.) This is a simple, well-known story that gives a mime much freedom in interpretation.

6. Often, the most effective way to stir up ideas for story lines is to let your imagination run free, a process called "free association." Write down any idea or word, then jot down the first thought that comes to-mind. This will produce another idea. Write that down, and continue in this way until you have a long list of ideas. This process may suggest a Mime plot that you can build into a pantomime.

Now choose the idea that you like best. Or, if you have not made up your mind, list the ideas that you think could lead to a well-constructed pantomime.

How to develop an outline

With an idea in mind, begin to write down possible story lines.

Ask yourself these questions:

Who does it?

Where does it happen?

What happens? What is the climax? What leads up to it; and what follows it?

How should the story end? Happy or sad? With a surprise ending or in a predictable way?

Take the time to sit back, daydream, and use free association. Your work on characterization should suggest a number of possible happenings and situations that you can now build into a story outline.

For example: *The Genie in the Lantern*

The word "genie" usually calls to mind the traditional image of a genie with folded arms and a turban, but further thought about "genie" will yield many ideas for a more complicated character and suggest a story line as well:

The traditional, inscrutable genie, turbaned, with arms folded.

A bumbling magician who puzzles over each incantation.

A servile, sleazy type, like the old villain of silent movies.

A tall, dark, handsome genie.

A fat, old, world-weary conjurer.

A cute, sprightly female genie, etc.

The mime or performance character should be the "finder" of the lantern. The possibilities for the three wishes are limitless—money, food, beauty, talent, love, travel, a big house, a new car, youth, jewelry, fame, good luck, etc.—and stir up a host of possible plot directions. If you let yourself imagine any of these possibilities, you can broaden the scope of your material.

The outline for *The Genie in the Lantern* could run as follows:

Performance Character (P.C.) goes for a walk, stumbles on lantern, rubs it (to clean it).

Genie appears and grants three wishes.

P.C. wishes for money.

Genie grants a flood of money which almost smothers P.C.

P.C. desperately swims through it and throws piles of money into audience.

P.C. makes second wish for food.

Genie grants a huge banquet table which P.C. proceeds to gorge on until he feels ill. Must take medicine.

P.C. is sad and disheartened and wishes for love.

Genie transforms into lover.

They go off arm in arm.

How to play a male or female genie, questions of blocking, depicting the three wishes, and how to show yourself clearly in the two roles of "genie" and "finder" can be worked out later, in rehearsal. The question at this point is whether you have a complete story with a beginning, middle, and ending.

What else is required?

Emotions. To flesh out an outline you should choose the emotion or emotional progression that conveys to the audience the effect you wish. Establish the emotion and tone, draw on it, then move on, keeping the flow of the pantomime going. At this point, you may bring a character you have developed earlier into play. If the character has any depth or complexity, you can work emotional reactions into your story line.

To bolster your confidence, make a list of the emotions the character must express to tell the story. Then, in rehearsal, you can fine tune the physical movements showing these emotions.

A mime stands on surest ground when he can recall familiar experiences and emotional scenes or experiences. If the drama requires the mime to feel pain, try to recreate that emotion from your past experiences, draw upon it, and apply it to your plot. In that way, you will convey the emotion more realistically. Or, recall the feeling of extreme joy, and relive that emotion as you perform your pantomime. In recreating an emotion, remember that the character in your script may have to react differently from the way you did originally.

Shy away from totally unfamiliar emotions. An audience may well detect an untrue or insincere emotional representation and quickly lose interest in your performance, or worse still, may become uneasy and not be caught up in the performance.

Humor. A surprise or unexpectedly funny ending will add a welcome twist to the story. If in the story of the *Genie in the Lantern*, your trademark character is a young female and you have characterized the genie as someone a young girl could be interested in, you have a built-in ending: After the girl's first two wishes result in disappointment, she asks for love. The genie suddenly "sees" her for the first time. He smiles and offers himself. She falls in love on the spot. The girl locks arms with the genie. "They" start to leave, but the girl remembers the lantern, stops, picks it up, kisses it, looks over her shoulder at the audience and winks, then happily marches offstage with the genie.

How to write a synopsis. You don't have to be a literary genius to set your ideas down on paper. Nor do you have to worry about the intricacies of dialogue; remember, traditional Mime is silent. With your outline in front of you, go back and flesh it out with short descriptions of the action, listing the sequence and progression of the plot. But don't create such intricate choreography that you will get bogged down in specific movements rather than the total effect of your story. Synopses of pantomimes are written so that in rehearsal the mime can add motion to the general story line, depending on his individual ability, skills, and interpretation.

Here is an example of a synopsis for a typical, intermediate level pantomime:

Title: Reflections of Age
Written by Matthew Straub
To be performed exclusively by Cindie Straub
Copyright 1980 Registration # PAU 232-635
Synopsis: An imaginary mirror serves as a frame for a pantomime.

Beginning as an *old woman*, the mime steps through the mirror, and depicts the various appearances of a woman as she progresses from infancy through old age. Coming back to the real world, she smiles her approval of her life, kicks her heels, and exits:

Action: The mime as an *old woman* shuffles onstage and proceeds wearily about her chores. She notices how dirty the mirror has become. As she cleans the glass, the surface vanishes and she finds, much to her surprise, that her hand can go through to the other side. Tentatively, she peeks through and finally, inquisitively, steps all the way through. (She may also fall through.)

Suddenly, she spins wildly about and comes to rest on the floor, now as *an infant.* The infant, crawling about, comes across her reflection in the mirror. She feels the "reflection" on the mirror and makes baby gestures and movements. Not sure of her discovery, she eventually loses interest and crawls offstage.

The mime skips back onstage as *a child.* Noticing the mirror, she begins studying her image. She prances about, fixes her pony tail, and watches herself, as if in a fantasy. Losing interest, she skips off.

The mime, now as *a teen-ager,* saunters back on. She postures in front of the mirror, trying out various poses, admiring herself. She examines her face, primps her hair, sucks in her cheeks. She tries different hair styles. Her fantasy is abruptly ended when her date comes to the door (offstage). She pats her hair one more time as she rushes offstage.

The mime now comes in as *a bride.* She sweeps up to the mirror, and excitedly yet in deep thought, adjusts veil, touches up her make-up, and picks up bridal bouquet. In the excitement, she drops the groom's ring. Frantically searching, she finds it, and with a distracted sigh, rushes offstage in a fluster.

The mime then enters as *a middle-aged woman.* She proceeds to pick things up off the floor and in exasperation "yells" offstage at her kids. Looking at the mirror, she blows on it and begins to clean it, and slowly notices her face. She studies the signs of age and smiles wanly at her reflection. Shrugging her shoulders, she continues cleaning and moves offstage.

The mime now shuffles on as *an old woman* with a cane. Approaching the mirror, she peers quizzically at her appearance. By furrowing her brow, she suggests deep thought; then, as she recalls the past, her face displays a range of emotions. Sighing, she shrugs, suggesting a return to a neutral mood and then, smiling, to contentment. She straightens her back and does a little dance step, kicking up her heels! With a wince, she chuckles, and hobbles offstage.

In this pantomime, *Reflections of Age*, there are two themes or ideas: Mirror and Age.

The plot starts from the first movement, when an old woman (who) hobbles up to a mirror (where); then she sets the direction of the plot with an unexpected twist by falling "through" the mirror and becoming a baby (what happens).

The rest of the story leads the audience through various age portrayals, as the mime performs physical movements characteristic to each age (what happens).

The plot is simple. It relies mainly on characterization. The device of "falling through a mirror" is well known to American and European audiences.

The plot is clear. Each age sequence has a "mini-ending." The story has its own inner logic.

The humor is quick and subtle, not drawn out.

The lifelong development of a woman, her attitude at each stage, and her final satisfaction with her life are conveyed through the emotional context of the pantomime.

The ending is amusing, brings a surprise, and is true to the character required by the plot.

This synopsis has summarized the story with happenings and emotions, but it has left the physical interpretation to the mime.

The success of this specific pantomime rests on the mime's ability to play the ages of womanhood cleverly and truthfully.

For a man, the mime could take the same synopsis and substitute appropriate masculine actions. For example:

An old man stands in front of the mirror, takes his glasses off, squints, then falls through the mirror.

A baby boy, played the same way as a female infant.

A boy with a baseball bat, throws a ball up, hits it and breaks a window.

A teen-age male keeps combing his hair, trying different hairstyles, shaves and cuts himself.

A nervous groom constantly fixes his boutonniere and fumbles for the bride's ring.

A middle-aged man, shaving notices his wrinkles, receding hairline, and bulging stomach.

The old man shrugs his shoulders and saunters off.

The Reflections of Age offers the audience humorous, sympathetic light entertainment. Yet is leave them with something to think about *after* the pantomime is over.

After you have written and polished your synopsis, check the manuscript for spelling errors and clumsy word constructions. Always type the manuscript to give it a polished and professional look.

COPYRIGHTS

Copyrights are the "rights" to the "copy" you write. Under Federal law, artistic creations are protected against unauthorized use. A copyright does not prevent someone else from using your material. Nor does the copyright office act as a police force to seek out abusers or punish them. It merely records the date of the copyright and describes the content of the material submitted.

You should copyright all your material.

Write to: Copyright Office
            Library of Congress
            Washington, D.C. 20599

Ask for form *PA* to receive the application and instructions. Fill out the PA form, then submit it with $10.00 and a typed copy of the title page, and synopsis of your pantomime. The script for the Synopsis and Action of *Reflections of Age* (on pages 102–104) were submitted to the Copyright Office in the form that they appear here.

UNIT 7

Rehearsal

Rehearsal

A PANTOMIME script (synopsis), described in Unit 6, gives basic guidelines for the mime, indicates the broad outline of the story, but leaves much of the development and "acting out" of the plot to the mime's ingenuity and skill in rehearsal. This unit discusses the essence of Mime performance: How can you transform the written words of the synopsis into the physical actions and gestures of a convincing pantomime performance?

STRUCTURE OF A PANTOMIME PERFORMANCE

Before actually beginning to rehearse, the mime should know the segments of a pantomime performance, and what should occur in each.

Beginning. The pantomime actually begins with the announcement of the title. This may be done with a sign, banner, flag, or a title card. A clever pantomime title will help focus the attention of the audience and make clear what the pantomime is going to be about, and what the audience can expect.

Once the title is given, the mime assumes the Beginning Position and "freezes" just long enough to signal the beginning of the pantomime. The first actions should be exaggerated to help establish a starting point for the pantomime and to set the tone and mood for the audience.

Development. The physical sequences that follow lead the audience through the various stages of the plot development—conflicts, range of appropriate emotional reactions, and resolutions—that make up the pantomime.

Without emotion, a story line may simply remain a series of unrelated physical movements displayed before an audience—similar to a gymnastic competition. The movements alone carry no theme, no feeling, and no characterization. A pantomime that is not developed beyond this level will quickly lose its audience. An emotional component must be added to give direction, meaning, and texture to the sequence of actions that is only the skeleton of a plot.

Humor and charm can also be added to the pantomime. Humor can be very subtle and sometimes not even consciously noticeable. A small movement, a facial expression—a smirk or a raised eyebrow—or a gesture of the hand, can "tone" a pose.

Ending. The ending serves two purposes: It wraps up the plot and signals the audience that the pantomime is over. The action should fall quickly from the climax to a definite close. The final movements of the plot should be exaggerated and end with a flair. After a pause, the mime steps out of character and bows.

Applause follows.

With the foregoing parts of a pantomime performance in mind, the mime is ready to rehearse his own pantomime.

Rehearsal

Since most of your performing places will probably be small, choose a rehearsal space that isn't too large, but large enough to work in. There should be room for a mirror large enough to reflect your whole body. Wear leotards and tights to allow for unencumbered movement.

Warm up, using all of your Isolation Exercises.

The procedure. Using the pantomime synopsis of *Reflections of Age* for our example, begin with the character of the *old woman*. To portray an old woman, use an aged position described on page 87. You may also give your character an imaginary cane.

Begin by moving toward an imaginary mirror. Remember to move the cane out first, then walk in a "shuffle fashion" up to the mirror.

Repeat until you have reached the mirror.

Stop and put a piece of tape on the floor where you want the imaginary mirror to be, to make sure the mirror is in the same place each time you approach it.

Repeat this shuffling sequence until you feel it is convincing and comfortable for you. Do not remove the tape on the floor until the rehearsal is completed.

Stand in front of the mirror. Lean forward (remember—you are holding a cane) and peer into the mirror. Now you must establish the fact that this is a "mirror." To do this, first put your cane down or lean it up against an imaginary wall. Remember to move in the character as the old woman (slowly). To make it very clear that you are looking into a mirror, squint at your image, straighten your clothes, and touch your face, observing how you look. Your eyes should constantly be looking into the mirror, focused on the part of the body you are looking at.

Now you must show the audience that you are going *through* the mirror.

This means you must touch the mirror again. There *must* be a *reason* for you as the old woman to touch the mirror. Let's say you see a smudge and want to clean it. You should show this by *slowly* taking a "handkerchief" out of your "pocket" (an old man would use his cuff), giving it a shake to open it, and (with fingers pressed together) wiping a small part of the mirror clean. But your hand pushes beyond the surface, and you fall through, winding up on the floor as an infant! This whole movement and transformation can be done with a simple spin of your body, dropping into a sitting position on the floor, but ending up about a foot on the other side, facing the back side of the mirror. You will still be looking into the mirror, but now from the opposite side.

You now begin to act as the new character, the *infant*. The synopsis calls for the infant to see her reflection in the mirror, and make baby gestures and movements, lose interest and crawl off stage. Your characterization research should give you ideas on how to portray an infant.

Continue to work through this pantomime, portraying each new character, the character's relationship to the mirror, and the transformation into the succeeding character.

Once you have completed the initial run-through, you must rehearse repeatedly until the pantomime is natural and movements flow smoothly together. If you make notes of your motions, remember that these can only be temporary aids. You should memorize the sequences as soon as possible, so you will feel completely at ease with them in your actual performance.

Using the rehearsal techniques for *Reflections of Age* as a model, take your own pantomime and put it into rehearsal. Solve each problem with clear, uncluttered motions. Do not add too many details. It will only confuse the audience. Make your point *clear*.

Example: If your pantomime calls for the character of a fisherman to put bait onto a hook, make it *simple*. Dig a hole, pull out a worm with one hand (wiggle your hand to show the worm's movement and/or show disgust with facial expressions), take the hook with the other hand and put the worm onto the hook.

DO NOT: open something (is it a tackle box?), fumble through a lot of hard-to-portray small objects (baits, hooks, sinkers?), drop the bait, look for it, find it, and then search the box for a hook. By the time you finally bait the hook, your audience will be lost. Always stick to the primary illusion.

MUSIC

Music can add dimension and richness to the pantomime, but it should always be in the background, and secondary to the mime's actions and movements.

Many people are uncomfortable with silence, and music minimizes this uneasiness. It also helps focus the audience's attention on the performance.

The pacing of rhythm of a pantomime can be improved with music. In performance, an inexperienced mime may rush the action, but carefully selected musical sections help keep the mime's performance within the intended time span and paced appropriately for the material. Of course, the mime does not have to move to the beat, unless he is portraying a dancer.

When choosing music, it is best to write the pantomime first, then find suitable music. Writing a drama to fit the music emphasizes the music and puts the mime in a supporting role, rather than vice versa. This becomes "silent acting."

Vocal music should be avoided, unless the mime intends merely to mime the words.

Instrumental classical music is often the best choice for a pantomime, because it is full of feeling and dramatization. A musician or music teacher should be able to make specific suggestions, though a mime may select appropriate music from some familiar tunes.

Example: Here is some possible music for *Reflections of Age*.

Persona	Music
old woman	"Old Gray Mare"
infant	"Rock-a-bye Baby"
child	"Good Ship Lollipop"
teen-ager	"Charleston"
bride	"Here Comes the Bride"
expectant mother	"In the Mood"
middle-aged woman	"Rock Around the Clock"
old woman	"Old Gray Mare," with a snappy ending.

Each suggested tune corresponds to the woman's role and the time in which she lived (i.e., a woman now in her seventies would have been dancing the "Charleston" in her teens).

If your pantomimes are to be performed outdoors, there are certain points to be considered when creating the material.

Sound systems are vulnerable to weather and close crowds, and there are also considerations of power supply and safety, sound quality, and background noises.

Using a live musician is a possibility, but coordination is a problem, and the musician may unintentionally upstage the mime. When a live musician is used, the mime loses some freedom to be spontaneous, since his motions must be coordinated with the music. Practice and rehearsals with mime and musician are necessary to make sure the production is as smooth as possible, and that the music highlights the mime's performance.

Even with the difficulties involved in using music outdoors, it can still enhance the pantomime and provide an engaging backdrop.

After the basic physical action sequences have been "mapped out," you have a pantomime, but it is not yet a polished or finished presentation. Extraneous movements must be eliminated; timing must be considered.

TIMING

Timing is the slowing or speeding up of actions and sequences within a particular pantomime. Your timing must always be in tune with the mood of the audience and the requirements of the material. If your timing is too fast as you move through an illusion, the audience will be confused. If it is too slow, they will become bored.

In the actual performance, although you are familiar with your material, as you should be, don't rush through automatically just because *you* understand it. Make each action seem spontaneous and fresh, no matter how many times you have presented it. Changing the material slightly for each performance will help keep it fresh for you. It would also be helpful for you to observe the timing techniques of your favorite actors, actresses, and comedians, and set the length and pacing of your show according to your own physical stamina.

LIGHTING

If you are working on a stage, you must arrange for lighting. The simplest lighting involves keeping the stage lighted during the pantomime, and then having the lighting technician turn the lights off at the end of each pantomime. This is done by writing a cue sheet for the technician.

Lighting terms
    CTB — Cut to black (turn lights off)
    FTB — Fade to black (dim lights to off)
    up   — lights on
    house — audience
    stage — stage area
    count — count "1, 2, 3," etc.

Example of a lighting cue sheet

```
Title:
   Show Time:
   Date:
```

MIME		LIGHTS
	–	8:00 pm House lights CTB
	–	Stage lights up
	–	
Mime enters, performs pantomime, bows twice	–	
	–	FTB, count 10, bring stage up
Mime enters, performs second pantomime, bows twice	–	
	–	FTB, count 10, bring stage up
	–	
etc.	–	

Any other lighting effects can be written on a cue sheet similar to the one above, and discussed in advance with the lighting technician.

After you have thoroughly rehearsed your pantomime, and the movements have become routine and polished, you are ready to present the pantomime to the audience.

UNIT 8

Make-up and Costume

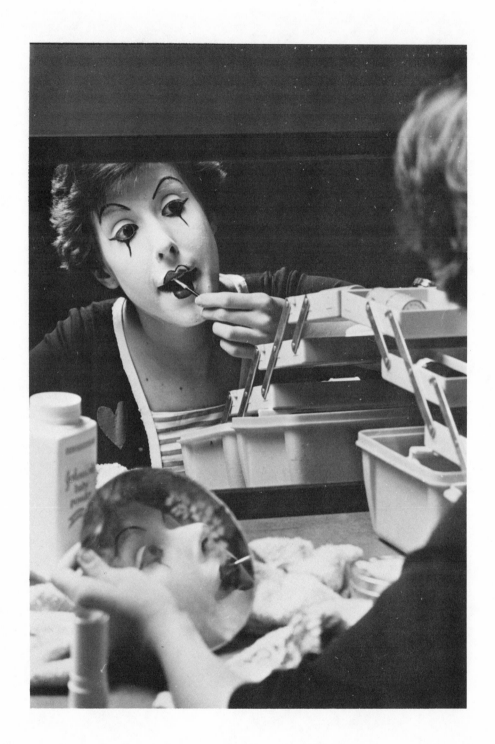

Make-up and Costume

MAKE-UP

MOST mimes choose to wear the *whiteface* make-up of traditional Mime. They are continuing a heritage of the early Greeks' use of stage masks to convey a "persona."

Roman mimes (and dancers) found it as expressive and more efficient to powder their faces with chalk dust.

The whiteface character of Pierrot, who enchanted French audiences in the late eighteenth century, is still a familiar figure today. After two hundred years, we now often see Pierrot's face as a decorative motif on jewelry, clothing, in pictures and various art forms.

Today, whiteface is associated in the popular mind with Mime. The predominant Mime school of the twentieth century, the French, features the whiteface character and has been widely popularized through the work of Marcel Marceau. Marceau's use of whiteface is an important theatrical device, which helps him create a striking and memorable image.

Whiteface focuses audience attention on the mime's face. The black lining around the eyes makes the eyes and eyebrows, as well as the mouth, visually project, and emphasizes the facial movements. White gloves, coordinated with the white make-up with black eyeliner, reinforces the focus on the face when set against the predominantly black costume of traditional Mime.

Each mime wishes to express his individual *style* (not characterization) by applying the basic Mime whiteface make-up in his own special way. With heavier eyebrows or decorative lines around the eyes or an individualistic shaping of the lips, the performer can create many different faces well within the "neutral" requirements of traditional Mime whiteface.

In stage work, the whiteface projects a clean, attention-riveting brightness. Under today's strong stage lights and follow spots, a mime can project the subtlest of facial movements to large audiences.

In Street Mime, an obvious device like whiteface identifies the Mime and distinguishes him from the crowd. The whiteface make-up here, as on the stage, draws attention to the mime's face and highlights his facial expressions during the performance.

The mime's neutral whiteface should not suggest any emotional characterization. Make-up that tries to show an audience in advance what to expect from the character is, by its nature, not Mime make-up, but is rather more in the nature of clown make-up or stage make-up for silent acting.

Make-up does not make a mime; skill as a performer does. The whiteface of traditional Mime is not a fundamental requirement for a pantomime, and some mimes often choose not to use it. However, some make-up *must* be used in order to avoid a washed-out look under strong stage lights, and mimes should learn the fundamentals of regular theatrical stage make-up (not whiteface) from a good theatrical make-up book, even if they choose not to use whiteface.

Whatever style of Mime make-up you choose, you should not try to use it to tell the story, or to give clues as to whether the character is good or bad, young or old, sad or happy. Its purpose is solely to help direct attention to the focal points of the face. The mime's story must come not from the make-up or costume (if any), but from the technique and prepared movements of Mime.

Make-up materials

A mime may choose either *oil-based* make-up, known as *greasepaint,* or *water-based* make-up called *pancake.*

For a professional look, greasepaint is preferred.

Here is a list of materials found in a professional mime's make-up kit:

(Use only professional make-up paints, no cosmetic substitutes.)

    pot of clown white grease
    black liner grease
    red grease
    applicators
    liner brushes
    theatrical white powder or baby powder (not cornstarch)
    powder brushes
    baby oil
    rags
    mirror

Make-up can be purchased in the water-based form. Powder and powder brush are not always necessary.

Any light, sturdy box with many compartments may be used to carry these make-up materials. (Fishing tackle boxes are most commonly used by professionals.)

Advantages of greasepaint

—lasts much longer and is therefore important for long Mime programs

—appears brighter, does not give a washed-out look under theatrical lighting

—features can be drawn on more precisely

—will not smear if applied properly

Disadvantages of greasepaint

—must be powdered to set

—must be removed with an oil-based remover (such as baby oil)

—may take longer to apply

Most experienced mimes consider pancake make-up an amateur approach to make-up. Because pancake is so easy to apply, however (similar to white shoe polish), some mimes may choose to use pancake for street work or children's shows.

Advantages of pancake make-up

—easy to apply, good for children and beginners

—easy to wash off (use water)

—sets without powder

Disadvantages of pancake make-up

—has a dull, washed-out look

—does not last very long, is absorbed quickly into skin, and fades

—easily smeared

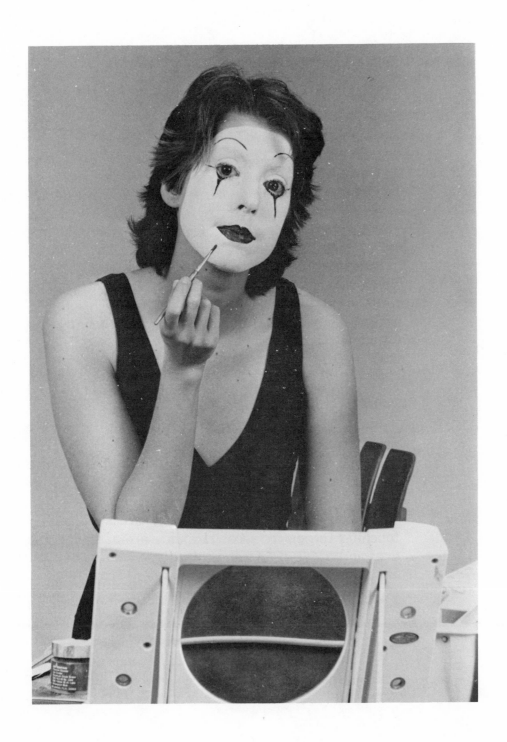

Application

For the basic Mime face, preferably using oil-based paints: First, pull all hair away from the face with bobby pins or a shower cap.

To apply clown white

Begin by dipping your first two fingers into the pot of clown white.

Starting across forehead, apply clown white generously downward until entire face is white. The downward stroke keeps all tiny facial hairs from standing up or creating "designs" in the paint. Cover entire face. Check nostrils, lips, area around the eyes, etc. Eyebrows should be completely blotted out. For those with very thick, black eyebrows, rub a *dry* bar of *white* soap over the eyebrows several times before applying the clown white.

Pat the entire face with the fingertips used to apply the clown white. This will even out the make-up and fill in facial lines and grooves on your face.

Put a generous amount of powder onto a powder puff.

Close eyes and mouth. Do not squint. The powder will not penetrate lines or wrinkles. Keep face relaxed. Powder it heavily, covering all areas.

Check for any remaining sticky areas by gently touching the entire face. Examine areas around the eyes and edges of face and chin. Repowder wet areas. Dust off excess powder with a powder brush.

To apply black liner

Dip the liner brush into the black liner pot (thin sparingly with baby oil, if necessary).

With brush, apply evenly around eyelids and, if you wish, extend lines ¼ to ½ inch beyond the edge of your eyelid.

Make a straight line, about one inch long, extending down from the middle of each lower eyelid.

Draw the Mime eyebrows thin, yet visible, with slight upward curve, ¼ inch above the normal eyebrow, along the top of the eyebrow muscle. This leaves enough space between the eye and the brow so that it is clearly visible.

Outline the edge of lips with black liner.

Outline the edge of the face, evenly, with black liner.

Powder all black lines heavily. Thoroughly brush off all excess powder so that the black lines are black as possible.

To apply red grease

Dip the lip brush into the red greasepaint.

Paint the lips, inside black lines (only after black line has been thoroughly powdered), covering the white with red.

Powder red heavily.

Brush off excess with powder brush until red is clearly visible.

You have just created the basic Mime face. This "created" face is used by hundreds of mimes everywhere and is a definite theatrical asset to the performance of Mime.

It can be gratifying for a mime to create his own face, to make it unique, different from all other mimes. Experiment with the make-up, using the techniques above, and fashion a face distinctly your own. Remember that you are refining your image, not creating a characterization; that comes from the skill of the Mime performance.

Exercises with Mime Make-Up

Practice the following exercises in front of a mirror, so that you can visualize your expressions as the audience will see them.

If your make-up begins to run or smear, apply more powder to set it. Brush off excess powder.

Create the following expressions using only your face.

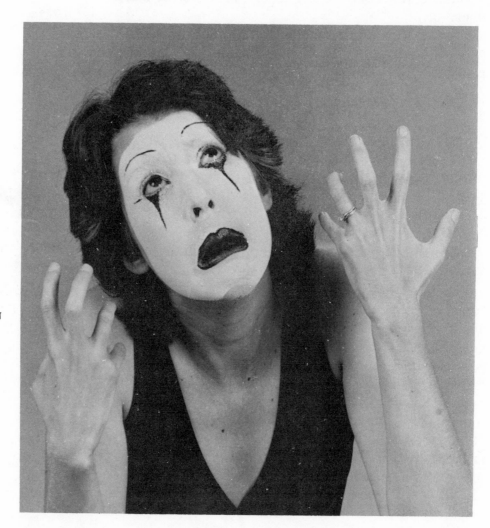

FRUSTRATION

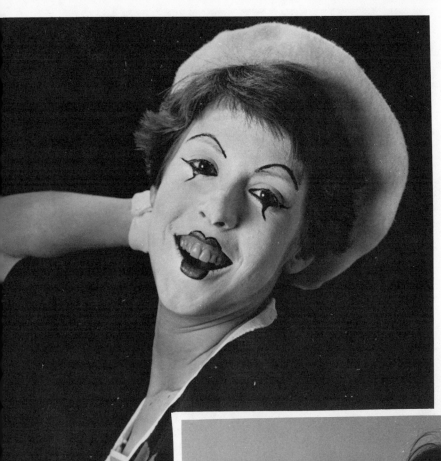

HAPPINESS

SNOBBERY

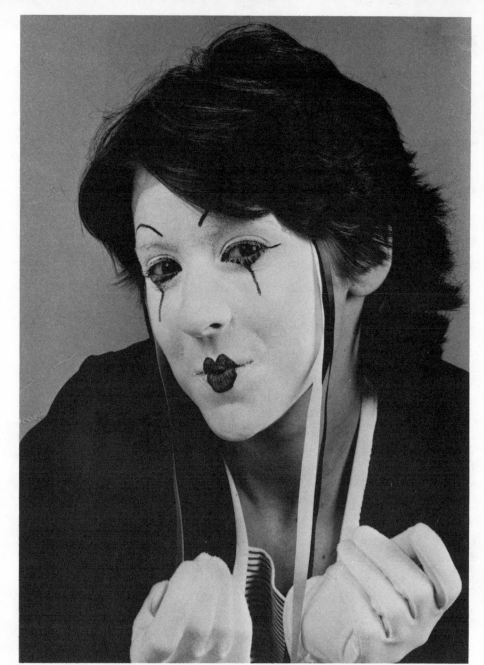

GREED

Each expression should be exaggerated to show clearly the emotion it is trying to convey.

Repeat the list, going smoothly from one emotion and expression to the next.

128

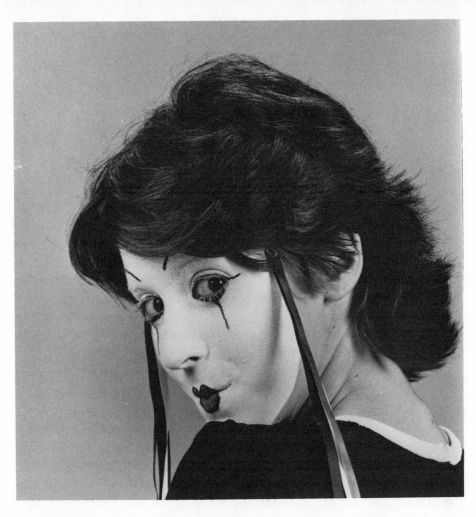

COPYRIGHT

You may wish to *copyright* your Mime face so that no other performer can use your original, carefully worked out, unique make-up ideas without your permission. Merely write a simple *story* about your performance character, including the exact details of your facial make-up. Mail it with a PA *application*, and a $10.00 application fee to:

Copyright Office
Library of Congress
Washington, D.C. 20559

Most professional mimes and all professional clowns copyright their "created" faces.

COSTUME

The forethought you give to your costume is an indication of your professionalism. Leotards and tights are usually for exercise, rehearsal, and warm-up, not for performance, though some professional mimes choose to wear unitards.

Costuming your character

The performer in a pantomime can actually be portraying three character levels simultaneously: the mime, the mime's trademark character, and the mime's trademark character in a specific role in the pantomime.

The character you are costuming here is your basic character (persona) as *the mime*.

To this basic costume, some *mime's trademark character* style accessories, such as gloves, a flower, a certain hat, etc., may be added.

In addition, you may add an item pertinent to the *mime's trademark character in a specific role:* a baker's hat, if a particular pantomime is about a baker. Make the addition small, so it will not clutter the image you are presenting to the audience. Remember: That is what the audience is watching: a mime creating an illusion.

Mime must remain an illusion. A mime playing a farmer should be wearing the basic mime costume with only a small suggestion of the farmer role—a red kerchief or a straw hat. A mime costumed *completely* as the character he is portraying—i.e., a farmer—changes Mime form to "silent acting," which, in addition to full costume, also depends on props and sets. The Mime illusion is then in the realm of standard theater.

A Mime costume, like whiteface, must enhance your performance, not overwhelm it. It should be closely fitting, but easy to get in and out of (no buttons), to keep body movements clearly visible. Your costume should have no more than three basic pieces, plus hat (if desired), gloves, and shoes.

The traditional and most recognizable outfit for Mime is composed of a red and white or black and white striped shirt and black pants, with or without suspenders. To this basic Mime outfit, you may add a unique touch or personal "trademark." Marcel Marceau wears a flower in his top hat, in addition to his own basic costume, to signify his special character, Mr. Bip. The audience knows immediately who this image is. But when out of the Mr. Bip character and doing one of his "pantomimes of styles," Marceau takes off the top hat and flower and uses only his basic Mime costume.

Hats make good and quickly identifiable trademarks. They don't alter the basic Mime look, are easy to change, easily seen from a distance, and define specific personalities or roles. They can be a part of your basic Mime personality or quickly indicate your role in a specific pantomime.

As indicated earlier, some mimes wear white gloves to enhance the formality of their basic Mime image. White gloves can be clearly seen and accentuate the whiteface. In street Mime, white gloves plus whiteface clearly separate the mime from the audience.

Shoes should be unobtrusive, with the color coordinated with the costume. Do not wear shoes that distract the viewers or detract from the Mime image.

Costume materials

Whether you buy or make your costume, you should consider these points:

The material you use for your costume should be strong, able to withstand lots of stretching, yet flexible enough to allow freedom of movement. To be practical, the material should be washable and colorfast, and it should not show perspiration stains.

Use a material that is easy to sew, so that repairs can be easily made.

Use material that will allow the body to breathe. Suggested fabrics are: Spandex, silky satin, gabardine, and possibly some knits. Avoid cotton, because it restrains movement and wrinkles easily.

A hat should be color–coordinated with the costume and be of the same material, if possible, unless it is an obvious and familiar symbol of a specific character, such as a fireman's hat.

White gloves should be cotton or nylon, easy to wash and bleach.

Ballet shoes may be worn on stage, but they are not durable and will quickly be worn out by street Mime. The best shoes to wear are gymnastic slippers with firm soles, or flexible-soled sneakers (not jogging shoes). Use shoes that can be redyed or polished.

Sources of costumes

For shirts and pants, try dance or skating supply stores and clothing stores.

Used hats and gloves may be found in thrift shops, yard sales, flea markets or you may, of course, buy new ones. Hats can also be cheaply made.

Shoes should be bought new at dance or gymnastic supply stores, or may be found in some department stores. Be sure to buy the correct color of polish, and plenty of it. Clean your shoes for every performance.

Final tips

1. Immaculate appearance is fundamental to good stage presence.

2. The make-up must be clean, evenly applied, with no runs or smears.

3. The costume should be well fitted, giving clean

lines to every movement. Wrinkles or bulkiness will dispel the illusion you have worked so hard to create.

4. Guard against telltale spots on the light-colored materials of your costume.

Hats should be securely fastened.

If you have designed a unique costume you wish to copyright, do it in the story form manner used for face make-up copyrights, described on page 129.

UNIT 9

Performance

136

Performance

THIS unit deals with different performance situations and how to prepare yourself for them.

AUDIENCES

An audience is not an enemy to be feared. An audience is merely a large collection of individuals. If you can comfortably perform for one person, why not a thousand? Is performing for a thousand people one thousand times more nerve-racking than performing for a single person? Certainly not, and that is the key to nonchalant performance: Treat each audience, no matter what the size, as a single person. Relate to this "person" as supportive, sympathetic, as in fact, most people are. This approach will lessen your nervousness and allow you to concentrate on your performance.

Some viewers react quickly; others more slowly. Most audiences are made up of both. Use this to your advantage by pausing long enough in your movements to allow the quick reactors to pull along the slower ones. Think of your portrayal as a conversation, and be sensitive to the listener.

A performer must "work" the audience. In a humorous pantomime, give the audience time to laugh. Before the laughter completely fades, add another laugh on top of it. Do the same again, carrying along and building on the original momentum.

Do not make abrupt pauses. Instead, slide into a pause by slowing down the action immediately before it. Hold the pause *almost* too long, then continue the action. This stylistic control holds the audience's attention.

THEATER PERFORMANCE

Mime audiences are usually knowledgeable about Mime as an art form. Therefore, you need give no explanation of what Mime is before you begin a theater performance. You might include a paragraph in the program giving your personal perspective on the art of Mime. Also include some information about yourself as well as a photo, if possible.

The program for a theater performance should list the titles of the pantomimes in order of their appearance.

Concentration is the key to a successful stage performance. Do not prejudge the audience or be offended by how *individual* people act or what you think they may be thinking. Concentrate only on your performance, move by move.

Each pantomime should have a definite, strong beginning and definite ending, with exaggerated movements. (See Unit 7, pages 109–110)

The arrangement and sequence of the various pantomimes within the program are important for the successful timing and tempo of a program. The relationship of the individual pantomimes helps determine the overall pace and the ability of the performer to keep the audience interested.

Start the show with a dramatic, attention-getting piece. It should be simple, direct, and energetic. Quieter, more subtle pantomimes may follow once the audience is accustomed to the nature and style of your performance. The final piece should be a sure crowd-pleaser and leave them wanting more. Present your most effective material in the first and last positions on your program. Perform your simpler pieces early in the program and the more abstract pieces later on.

STREET PERFORMANCE

The street mime has the task (and the freedom!) of selecting and drawing a responsive audience from the passersby.

First and foremost, pick a good location. A street corner with little pedestrian traffic is hardly a place to draw a crowd. You must study each possible site for the number and types of people likely to be present and the amount of attention you might expect.

Where you situate yourself will also depend on the time and the day of the week. (Be aware of how the time of day affects the attitudes of the passersby.) A late afternoon street show may quickly be crowded with rush-hour commuters, and then street traffic will dissipate during the supper hour. What works at one time may be a disaster fifteen minutes later. Try to gauge the crowd.

Consider these four points when choosing a street location that will draw an audience:

Time: The hour, day, proximity to eating time, and probable weather conditions.

Mood: People relax at lunch time, while window shopping, on the weekend, and when on vacation.

Environment: Choose a site free from construction and heavy traffic distractions. Look for areas that are natural "mini-amphitheaters."

Pedestrian traffic: Look for a large, slow-moving stream of people.

Use these six attention-getters for drawing an audience:

Music: Either background music or music suited to your performance will draw attention.

The Wall: This Mime trademark works every time and can be used when you want to travel from one location to the next.

The Flower: Give this "gift" to test a potential participant's reaction.

The Walk: Arouse onlookers' curiosity as you energetically go nowhere. "Stop" to do a skit and then go on.

The Climb: Lure passing onlookers into looking up as you climb to an ever-receding "object."

The Statue: This absolutely motionless pose will go unnoticed by some people, startle others, and create a crowd when some individuals stop to watch and others stop to see what they are looking at.

If you have chosen a good time and location, your adeptly performed attention-getters will surely draw a crowd.

Skits

After you have gathered a crowd, you can continue to use some of the skits you used to get their attention, but you should enlarge on the action. Improvisation is the core of a street mime's performance. You can use the following skits as your points of departure.

The Wall: As you move along, stop to open doors and windows. Reach through to shake hands, blow a kiss, etc. At each "window," you have a new person to work with and a new situation to create.

William Tell: Place a Mime apple on someone's head, step back and shoot a Mime arrow at the "apple," then (having missed your aim) rush to another person and pull the arrow from the second person's forehead. Grab the "apple" from the first person, take a bite, and throw it into a trash container.

The Statue: Try standing among real mannikins in a store. Choose an uncrowded place. Your aim is not to draw a large crowd for a show. The point is to make people wonder whether you are real or not. Assume a comfortable pose that you can hold for a long time. Use diaphragmatic breathing. Do not move.

When you tire, abruptly change position, staying in character. Avoid people who may try to touch you. Raise your hand and motion, no, no! If they persist, frown and push away their hands. Some people will try to make you smile. This harmless activity can be countered by focusing on a distant object or concentrating on a sad event. It works!

The Sword Fighter: Have a sword fight behind someone's back. If your victim starts to catch on, nonchalantly switch to someone else.

Gifts: Blow balloons for children. Complete the illusion by tying it to their wrists and giving it a pat! Make it burst, or let it escape and watch it float away.

Pick flowers and put them in women's hair and men's lapels.

Pick apples, offer a bite to others and then pull a wiggling worm out of the apple.

Use the other Moving Illusions suggested in Unit 4.

By using these basic illusions, you can improvise on the spur of the moment. Experiment with your surroundings. Develop your own repertoire of effective improvisations.

One final word about children in the crowd. If there is a child who is scared of your costume and appearance, let him touch your make-up. Kneel and have the parent touch your make-up, if need be. The child will probably follow. If not, and the child remains scared, smile and blow a kiss, then move on.

If the parent is unintentionally inhibiting a child's response, pleasantly draw the child away from the immediate zone of the parent. Indicate that something "special" is going to happen. Position the child so that he is facing away from his parent and proceed.

CHILDREN'S AND OTHER INFORMAL SHOWS

Children's shows and informal shows, such as those for church groups, banquets, and other seated groups not in a theater, are a sizable part of many mimes' performing schedules. These groups can include a large proportion of children and many individuals who may not know what Mime is. These shows require and deserve special attention.

When asked to give a children's show, find out the age range, the number of children in the audience, the time of the performance (around lunch time, dinner), and the sort of place the performance area is. Don't leave anything to chance.

These shows (children's and adults' alike) must be obvious—so that everyone understands what's going on. Your costume must clearly set you off as a performer; don't wear a mottled assortment of street clothes. Use make-up to make your appearance "special" and arouse the viewers' curiosity.

Your pantomime titles must be clear and somehow suggest each plot.

Your performance must have a definite beginning and a *definite* ending. Give a final bow.

It enhances the performance to have a knowledgeable person (Master of Ceremonies or M.C.) introduce the show with a brief explanation of what Mime is. The M.C. may also give a brief synopsis of the pantomime to be presented, but this should not tell the entire story.

For children's shows, the M.C. should also stress that Mime is a silent art form, and that everyone should remain quiet, unless asked by the mime to call out responses.

For children, a good performance area takes care of much of the discipline. If you are careful about the advance arrangements and set-up, you will avoid many problems. If things are left to chance, many hidden distractions may arise to mar the performance. Since children are easily influenced by their immediate environment, remove as many distractions as possible beforehand.

If there are adults in the audience, bring the children to the front, close to you and away from the adults, who often curb their natural enthusiasm or explain every move.

Strategically position the ushers. Talk to them beforehand and explain that their role is to support the performer, not to be policemen and stifle audience enthusiasm. For the very young, an usher (or teacher) may act as a "prompter" who leads the applause and laughter.

The younger the audience, the simpler the story line must be.

Three- and four-year-olds can sit for 10 to 20 minutes.

Five- to eight-year-olds can handle a 20- to 25-minute performance.

Children eight years or older may enjoy a show of up to 45 minutes long.

Avoid having your audience, children or adults,

seated at tables, where they can be easily distracted by other people at their table or by refreshments in front of them. If they are seated in an auditorium, gather them in a close group at the front, to create an intimate atmosphere. Remember to keep your performing zone clear, because people may tend to crowd the "stage" area.

As a finale for any group with children in it, do a humorous skit with a surprise ending. *The Wedding* skit works well and draws a tumultuous reaction from children and adults alike. Choose a boy and a girl. Have them hold hands, bless them, and show them that they have to exchange "rings." As you ask them to kiss, it will quickly dawn on them, amid the general laughter, that they have been set up. Then, bow and exit during the resulting applause.

Afterword

MIME AS A CAREER

PEOPLE studying Mime for performance have obviously done so for reasons other than making money. But as you become confident as a performer, you may naturally ask, "Can I make a living at this?"

Because the American public in general does not understand what true Mime is, full-time, steady jobs as mimes are—regrettably—rare. (Television presentations of true Mime are changing this—slowly.) As of January 1984, however, a newly organized group, The National Mime Association, Davis-Elkins College, Elkins, West Virginia 26241, began publishing a newsletter with job listings and other information regarding the Mime field.

If you are in college, study theater and get as much stage experience as possible. Also take dance classes to keep your body toned and disciplined. Develop your skills in such general theater arts as make-up, staging, costuming, and lighting, under the guidance of professionals. At some point, you should study under a professional mime, or one who has had extensive experience in this specialized and demanding art form.

As an aspiring mime, you may devote yourself to a full-time career in Mime, but unless you have enough money to support yourself, working part-time is more realistic. In fact, most performing mimes hold full-time jobs in related or even completely different fields, and perform on the side when the opportunity arises. If possible, this secondary career should have flexible hours and not be too demanding on your time and energy.

American mimes, whether superstars or street performers, must be "self-promoting." You must create your own jobs. People who book entertainment do not automatically think of Mime, so it's your job to promote yourself, and present them with a number of situations in which they can use your services.

As a free-lance mime, your possible markets are: birthday parties, carnivals, department store promotions, nursery school shows, country club functions, art festivals, holiday events, art gallery openings, fund raisers, convention entertainment, cocktail parties, bar and bat mitzvahs, receptions, school assembly programs, banquets, civic events, children's theaters, YMCAs and YWCAs, camps, etc.

Understand the importance of good publicity. Business cards, fliers, or brochures should be printed and distributed to potential groups.

Become a direct-mail expert. Learn about the U.S. Post Office's bulk rate mailing rates. Refer to your library's copy of the *Thomas Registry of American Manufacturers* (Thomas Publishing Company) under LISTS: Mailing for professional help, or personally assemble mailing lists of churches, civic groups, professional associations, art councils, banquet halls, convention centers, etc., from the Yellow Pages, covering a hundred-mile radius from where you live.

Design a logo or trademark for your stationery, business cards and advertising brochures—something visually unique and memorable.

Call your local newspaper and ask them to send out a photographer whenever you perform, and be sure to keep a file of any newspaper clippings of your performances. These will be part of the portfolio that you'll show potential clients, to give them confidence in your abilities. Also include professionally photographed glossy photos of yourself—in mime poses, during performance, etc.

When trying to determine how much to charge for your performances, find out what other local acts charge. Since you are a solo performer, your fee may be lower than that charged by groups. You can give free performances, but realize that these will probably only lead to requests for more free performances.

When talking to potential clients, emphasize your flexibility and mobility. Remind them that you require no electrical outlets, props, scenery, stage, or lights—all you need is an audience. Your act comes "hassle-free."

Keep in touch with groups or individuals for whom you've performed, reminding them that you're available, and offering them "something new and even better than before." Be prepared to do both street Mime and stage shows to accommodate your clients.

Draw up simple contracts with your clients, giving the details of your performance and the price charged, so there will be no misunderstandings.

GLOSSARY

ACTION—A body movement or series of body movements that conveys an idea or opinion.

ANIMATE—To give life to.

BODY LANGUAGE—Body movement or posture that reflects a person's unconscious attitudes, i.e., tightly folded arms or legs may indicate a person who feels he must protect himself.

CHARACTER—The qualities, personality and temperament that distinguish one person from another; the personal attitudes one builds through life, composed of beliefs, feelings, and behavior patterns.

CHARACTERIZATION—The process of researching and composing a personality and character for a fictional role and choosing the gestures and body and facial movements to portray it.

COPYRIGHT—A form of protection provided by the laws of the United States to the authors of "original works of authorship" including literary, dramatic, musical and artistic works.

DIAPHRAGM—The partition of muscles and tendons between chest cavity and abdominal cavity.

DIAPHRAGMATIC BREATHING—Inhaling and exhaling from the diaphragm.

DOWNSTAGE—At or toward the front of the stage.

EMOTIONAL SIGNATURE—A physical representation of a character trait.

ENVIRONMENT—The total of all physical factors in a performing situation, including all surrounding influences, whether a planned part of the performance or not.

EXTENSION—The straightening of an arm or leg away from the body.

FOCAL POINT—In performance, the spot most people in an audience are looking at at any given time.

GESTURE—A physical expression or movement given with hands or feet to emphasize, highlight, or enhance the action.

ILLUSION—The creation of an imaginary object or action using stylized techniques.

IMPROVISATION—The creation of a spontaneous sequence, story, or pantomime.

ISOLATION—A technical exercise designed to work individual parts of the body.

MIME—When the word is capitalized, it refers to a system of physical technique and mental attitudes designed to give a performer understanding and control of his body; the theatrical art form that "speaks" with the body instead of the voice, indicating the personality, character, and plot of a pantomime script by physical gestures and movements only. When the word is in lower case (mime), it refers to a performer in the art form of Mime. A mime develops such skills as complete body control, and can create the illusions of weight, motion, and tension, as well as indicate personality and character of a chosen role. With this proficiency, a mime can express all manner of stories, emotions, and ideas, unaided by props, sets, or the spoken word.

MOTIVATION—The reason for a character's drive or actions.

NEUTRAL POSITION—The basic body position: standing in an upright position, expressing no feeling, thought, or motion; relaxed.

PANTOMIME—A script or dramatic program without words that the mime creates and performs, using the techniques of Mime.

PERSONA—The personality created by the performer; the "mask" of the characterization.

PERSONALITY—That part of a characterization that portrays the social aspects of the role and its use in interpersonal relations.

PLAYWRITING—The process whereby a playwright constructs and writes a play or pantomime.

PLAYWRIGHT—The "maker of plays"; the person who creates or writes a play or pantomime.

PROGRESSION—A sequence in which plot development or characterization development occurs.

REPRESENTATION—A portrayal, characterization, or an illusion, presented by a mime to depict "real" persons, objects, or events.

ROLE—The part a mime plays in a pantomime.

SEQUENCE—A predetermined, continuous succession of actions or illusions; a series of events following a plan.

STANCE—A body position indicating an attitude, personality, or character; a pose.

TECHNIQUE—A formalized method of Mime based on the study of body movement; a series of muscle, body position, and progressive exercises designed to help a mime gain control of the body and make actions predictable; the practiced skill resulting from study of a formal method.

TENSION—A tightening of specific muscles to add emphasis to an illusion.

UPSTAGE—At or toward the back of the stage.

WHITEFACE—Mime make-up, either greasepaint or pancake make-up, which covers the entire face and incorporates black, stylized lines drawn around the eyes and mouth, with painted red lips; designed to highlight the mime's facial expressions.

WALKS—Frontal: Mime Walk performed directly facing the audience. Profile: Mime Walk performed on any diagonal to the audience.

Index